Ben on C

By the same author

*The Mercury Cup*

*Ben and Blackbeard*

T. R. BURCH

# Ben on Cole's Hill

*Illustrated by Susan Neale*

A DRAGON BOOK

**GRANADA**
London Toronto Sydney New York

Published by Granada Publishing Limited in 1983

ISBN 0 583 30615 2



Granada Publishing Limited
Frogmore, St Albans, Herts AL2 2NF
and
36 Golden Square, London W1R 4AH
515 Madison Avenue, New York, NY 10022, USA
117 York Street, Sydney, NSW 2000, Australia
60 International Blvd, Rexdale, Ontario, R9W 6J2, Canada
61 Beach Road, Auckland, New Zealand

Reproduced, printed and bound in Great Britain by
Hazell Watson & Viney Ltd, Aylesbury, Bucks
Set in Plantin

## *Chapter One*

It was so quiet that the footsteps sounded like the thud of a hammer on wood. Ben stopped, listened, watched. All around him lay the thick blanket of snow which had started to fall an hour ago and had now made all the things he knew impossible to recognize. He was up on Cole's Hill, but which direction he had to take in order to reach home he had no idea. The sky was a dull grey, everything else white and silent, and a mist was closing in, so that he could no longer see the earth ramparts which ran round the top of the hill.

He was alone, and he was cold. He pulled the anorak round his head, but his ears still tingled with the biting wind, and his fingers hurt. He pushed his hands deep into his pockets.

The footsteps had stopped now.

'Isobel?' he called out. The sound of his voice was muffled in the mist-soaked air.

Just like Isobel to leave him when for once he needed her. She'd said something about going home and getting the tea ready, and he had hardly bothered to say goodbye. She would be sitting there now, she and Jane, toasting bread in front of a roaring fire.

Ben shivered.

It was odd about those footsteps. He could have sworn he had heard them, slow but distinct, fearful in the falling silence of the snow. Ben bent down, packed snow into an icy ball, waited. If it *was* Isobel stamping about up here on Cole's Hill, she'd have something to remember it by.

But it wasn't Isobel.

He heard them again, and he knew as well as he knew anything that Isobel would never walk like that. Ben whipped round, his fist full of snow. The wind seized his breath, made him gasp. He fell to his knees, rolled into a dell, lay still.

There were three of them. He had caught only a glimpse of them as the storm drove the snowflakes into his eyes. It was as though the wind had lifted the edge of a curtain and then dropped it again before he could see any more. Just three dark figures, two tall ones and somebody shorter and fatter, hidden in long dark coats which flapped at their legs and dribbled snow against their boots.

Slowly Ben crawled to the edge of the dell and looked across the thirty yards of whiteness as far as his eyes could reach. The men had gone now, and the sound of the footsteps had faded. Ben pushed the fear he had felt into the back of his mind and stood up. Like him, they had been out walking on the hills and got caught by the suddenness of the blizzard. One of them had been carrying something: they might have been out after rabbits, or a few pigeons from the woods which clung to the lower slopes of the hill. Unlike him, however, they had not lost their way. Their steps had been firm and sure. Three men who knew where they were going. He could follow them – easy enough in the snow – ask the way. They might even have a car parked somewhere close, and he could hitch a lift. The sooner he got home the better, or Isobel and Jane would have eaten all the toast.

The footsteps were easy to find, easy to follow. He realized that he was humming a verse of Good King Wenceslas, and he grinned. They'd all be singing it in a week's time when Christmas came.

'In his master's steps he trod, Where the snow lay dinted—'

Suddenly Ben stopped. Something dark and square and ghostly swam out of the flying snow and then was lost again. It was a moment or two before he remembered. The shepherd's hut.

Cole's Hill was a bare stretch of grassy down, surrounded by ditches and ramparts which people said had been there before the Romans came. No trees grew on its flattened top, only an occasional patch of prickly gorse or bramble. No houses, only the black and empty hut which once had been used by a shepherd when the sheep were allowed to roam wild. And that was years ago.

Ben was pleased with himself. He knew where he was now, and he could almost smell the toast, even if there was still at least a mile to go. He was about to turn and run when he heard something that made his hair prickle against the hood of his anorak.

'*There's enough stuff here to blow us all to kingdom come.*'

'*Then you be careful where you put your fag-ends, Jed.*'

'*This stuff needs a detonator, you fool, not a match.*'

'*And that's what it's going to have, all wired up and as sweet as a Christmas tree. You can trust your Uncle Sam.*'

Ben was drawn to those voices. Three men striding over the downs carrying something that looked like a crate, settling in at the shepherd's hut and gossiping idly about explosives and detonators and kingdom come. Ben wanted to know more.

He was ten yards from the hut. The trail of kicked and flattened snow led round the corner to a door which Ben knew had no lock but only a rusty iron latch. The only window, small and shuttered, was also on the far side. Ben began to move softly into the shadows of the hut. Snow lay thick on the sloping roof and lined each separate plank in the walls.

*'Keep that lamp down until I've got these windows fixed.'*

*'OK, Sam. Nobody's going to see us up here on a night like this, not even from a chopper.'*

*'Do as you're told.'*

*'OK, OK.'*

Wood slammed and a bolt squealed. The voices now were only a murmur and no words came to Ben's ears. Disappointed, he dropped to his knees, meaning to crawl round to the front of the hut, but he was brought to a sudden stop by something which sprang out at him from the wooden wall, like a red fiery eye. Ben grinned as he recognized it for what it was, a knot-hole an inch across, and convenient for listening.

*'How long do we stay here, Sam?'*

*'Till the job's done.'*

*'But that's two days –'*

*'Can't you stand the pace, Jed? All right, we'll let you out for a smoke every so often. The boss said this was the place to set it all up, so this is where we stay.'*

*'I don't like this snow.'*

*'Very pretty, very Christmassy. The carols'll make it sound even better. Nobody will dare come up here, not even his nibs, the one and only very important target. He'll be down there on the road, thinking all's well. He won't know anything else.'*

Somebody laughed. Boots scraped on uneven planks. Ben applied one eye to the knot-hole. A pity it was so low in the wall – all he could see was large snow-whitened boots, two pairs of them, one with a band of grubby yellow round the tops.

Ben tried to see more, considered enlarging the hole with his finger, thought better of it. He'd have liked to see their faces, though. It might have helped to know what sort of men they were, and what they looked like. All he had seen before was their backs, bent into the wind, long coats, and a crate. And all he could see now was two pairs of rubber boots. He wished he knew where the third pair was.

Ben's attention was so fixed on the little knot-hole that he didn't hear the scratch of the door being opened or the soft thud of feet on fallen snow. It was the smell of a cigarette that gave him the first warning. Someone had come out of the sheperd's hut and was prowling in the last light of the evening. Ben's muscles froze. If the man came round the corner, he was bound to see him. Ben's clothes were a dark blue, and round his neck was twisted a red woollen scarf. He had time to think that he must look like a ragged Union Jack, trodden into the snow and forgotten.

Then the feet thudded again, a few swift kicks against the rooting boards at the front of the hut. A man doesn't kick the snow off his boots unless he's going inside, Ben thought, and the breath came from his nostrils like smoke in the misty air.

'*Hey, Jed!*'

'*Yeah?*'

'*Come and look at this.*'

A confused mixture of chairs scraping and feet thumping and words muttered. Again Ben held his breath. Had he been seen? He pressed his body into the shadow of the hut and hoped for the best.

'*Looks lovely, doesn't it?*'

'*You brought me out here to look at the stars?*'

One man swore; another stamped his feet, blew on his chilled hands. Ben heard the swish of the door over the snow and thought he was safe. He left a second or two, then he was up and running, making his strides long, catching his breath from the wind which whistled past his cheeks and his ears. Then he stumbled, ran on, stumbled again, and his mouth was full of snow, and his hands were scrabbling at the white powdery surface which refused to support him, and the air came out of his lungs in a squeal.

Ben lay still. He knew that somebody had heard the noise, was already thudding towards him, was almost on him. He

heard somebody shout, and just in time his muscles obeyed him. Pulling himself to his knees, he glanced round, saw something monstrous and black like a great bird of prey swooping down to seize him. As the figure stooped, Ben rose. His head butted into the man's stomach, and his fists flailed harmlessly against his chest. Strong hands clawed at his anorak. Struggling and twisting, he tore himself free, staggered three steps, then ran. He didn't dare turn round to see if he was being chased. Blind panic led him to the earth ditches at the edge of the hill. He scrambled down, then up, then down again, his fingers trying to find a purchase in the snow-covered tussocks of grass, then he was rolling, over and over, down the steep side of Cole's Hill, unable to stop or control his descent until his legs hit a tree and his face buried itself in a drift and the snow covered him.

For a moment he thought he had broken an arm, so biting was the pain which froze his wrist. He moved his fingers, found the flint whose sharp edge had scraped his skin, and sighed. It took more than a stone like a knife to put him out of action.

The snow fell, fluttered, settled. He was out of the wind down here among the trees, but it was piercingly cold. Shivers crawled along his legs and up his back. He tried to pull his anorak round him and realized that he had left it in the grasp of the man on the hill. There was going to be trouble about that.

Slowly he sat up. Utter silence surrounded him, and a mist like cotton wool. Not even a twig stirred in the belt of trees which skirted the lower slopes of Cole's Hill. Peace. Ben watched and waited.

It was as he heaved himself at last to his feet that he heard a branch crack, not ten yards away, with a noise like a rifle-shot.

## *Chapter Two*

Ben's immediate thought was to run, but he pushed his panic to the back of his head and concentrated his attention on the direction from which the cracking branch had sounded. He tried to keep his shivering still and his breath quiet while he listened for a repetition of the noise which had made his senses kick like a mule.

Slowly he put one foot to the right and eased his body from behind the tree so that he had a wider view. The columns of the trees rose like grim still ghosts from a bed of gleaming white, and clean lines of snow defined each black branch. Ben's eyes tried to pierce the gloom and shadows, but nothing moved except the few flakes which swam eerily down to find a resting-place.

Ben was annoyed. He was cold and tired and hungry, and he was fed up with playing silly games. He hadn't done anything wrong, and he wasn't going to be bullied by three great brutes whom he had never seen before and didn't want to see again. He was going to march out into the open and dare them to come and get him.

But somehow his legs refused to move. If only he could see where they were, he thought . . . If only he could be sure they'd gone away, back to the hut on Cole's Hill, or wherever they'd come from . . . Then he could go home and have his tea.

He willed his legs to move, and he stepped softly into the shallow snow. There was less of it here under the trees, and he could see the outlines of dead branches on the ground and patches of grass. His eye caught a slight movement at the edge of the little clearing in front of him, but he no longer cared. Let 'em all come, he said to himself, and hoped they wouldn't.

The movement became a body, and the body produced a voice.

'Ben! Come *on*!'

He might have known, he reflected. Isobel . . . Even if she was only a year older than Ben, she liked to think she was in charge. Particularly now.

'Just like you,' he muttered. 'Clattering about and frightening everything.'

'I didn't mean to scare you.'

'Not me.' Ben was contemptuous. 'There's a badger lives in these woods. I was waiting for him. He won't come now, though, not after all this fuss. Have you got tea ready?'

Isobel tossed the long fair hair from her face. 'Hours ago. Jane's eaten nearly everything.'

'Typical.'

Jane was Ben's younger sister, a bookworm of a girl whose eyes rarely bothered with anything except printed words. She would have had all the toast, and not even noticed. Ben scraped patterns in the snow with one foot.

'Seen anyone about?' Offhand, idle, curious, in order not to worry her.

'Not even a badger.'

Ben strolled across the clearing. 'I'm hungry,' he announced. 'Come on.'

He felt better when he had his feet in front of the fire with a toasting fork in one hand and a piece of toast dripping butter in the other. He took no notice of Isobel's mother-like complaints: he was used to it, and he'd heard it all before. Jane was curled up on the rug reading, and that was normal, too. Ben put out a foot and stirred her into life.

'She's talking to you,' he remarked.

'You'd better change your socks,' was all Jane replied. 'They're wet through, and you'll catch your death of cold.'

'Don't you start. And, anyway, colds are caught from

germs, not wet feet. They'll dry in front of the fire.'

Jane glanced up with withering contempt. 'Men,' she remarked. 'You wouldn't say that if your mother was here.'

Ben began to feel besieged. He wiggled his toes in front of the fire. His socks *were* wet, true enough, but he was not going to be brow-beaten by a gang of women, especially when they were right. He tried to change the subject.

'Bel, have you ever seen anyone up on Cole's Hill?'

'No. Have you?'

'This evening. You know that old shepherd's hut? Three men have taken it over, two tall guys and one short and fat.'

Isobel looked worried. 'Taken it over?'

'I didn't like what I heard much. They were talking about blowing things up and detonators.'

'Mining engineers,' Jane suggested, but Ben squashed her with a look.

'Your mother ought to be here,' Isobel said.

'She's yours as well,' Ben reminded her reasonably. Isobel always tried to be the ruler when their mother had to go away. She had gone north this morning to visit Gran for a few days, leaving them to the care of Beryl.

Isobel seemed to know what he was thinking. 'Beryl rang half an hour ago. Said she couldn't get through. The snow's turned to ice on the road from the farm. She told me to remind you to wash.'

Ben ignored this. 'What's for supper?'

'Sausages and baked beans.'

'Don't forget the bread and butter.'

'You can see to that yourself, pig.'

Ben licked his buttery fingers and wiped them down his jeans. Isobel threw him a look.

'Where's your anorak?' she demanded.

Ben sighed. 'Somewhere.'

'You've lost it, haven't you?'

'I'll come and open the tin of beans for you,' Ben offered, but Isobel was not to be diverted.

'If you've left it lying around, somebody will probably return it,' she said. 'It's got your name and address in it, hasn't it?'

'Blast,' Ben said softly, and he gazed into the depths of the fire. He's forgotten those labels on his clothes, and there wasn't much chance that those great hulking brutes up at the hut were unable to read. 'Blast!'

'You ought to be grateful,' Isobel told him. 'Your other one's filthy.'

'It'll do.'

'It'll have to, because I don't intend to wash it.' Isobel slammed the door into the kitchen. Ben could hear her rattling cutlery and saucepans. He went on looking into the fire and thinking of the words he had heard through the knot-hole. How much did they mean?

Jane put a piece of paper in the book, closed it, and turned to the fire, hugging her knees. 'Let Bel get on with it,' she

said. 'She likes being the little mother, and she's not a bad cook. Not really. What were they like?'

'Who?'

'Your thugs on Cole's Hill.'

Ben shrugged. 'Ordinary. All muffled up. One might have had a moustache. Hard to tell. Not much light, and no time.'

'Recognize them? Thugs in books always have distinguishing marks, like a white scar running all the way down the side of their faces, or one green eye and one brown, or completely bald heads.'

'No such luck. Two tall, and one short, that's all.'

'Clothes?'

'Jeans and coats, like everybody else. Anyway, we'll probably never see them again.'

'What about the explosions? Who are they trying to explode?'

'They didn't tell me,' Ben said irritably. 'Somebody local. The vicar? The woman who runs your Brownies?'

Jane giggled. 'She's too tough. What did they sound like? Irish?'

Ben looked up quickly. 'Why Irish? It's a bit off the beaten track for the IRA.'

'You never know. Somebody passing through? Royalty, or Arab sheiks, or even the Prime Minister.'

Ben snorted in disgust. 'Imagination, Jane. Don't you let Bel hear you say that, or she'd never let—' Ben broke off as Isobel pushed her head round the door.

'In the absence of help,' she remarked sarcastically, 'I got supper myself.'

'Nice of you, Bel.'

'Put the guard round the fire, Jane, and Ben, put your shoes on. I'm not eating at the same table as you with your smelly damp socks.'

'Yes, ma'am.'

The sausages were well done, just the way Ben liked

them, with a covering of crisp dark skin. 'I like to know they're dead,' he said, plastering everything with tomato sauce. 'What's on telly tonight?'

'Cops and robbers,' Jane said. Jane always knew necessary facts. 'Probably with Irish accents.'

Isobel looked up in surprise. 'Why Irish?'

'Jane's joke.' Ben explained without much hope of being believed. Had those men on Cole's Hill spoken like St Michael, the old tramp who walked the local roads and who (Ben liked to think) was one of his particular friends? Now, there was an Irish accent for you! Ben had often suspected that St Michael made it even more obvious than nature intended, but the three men hadn't sounded anything like that. It was difficult to remember now. His attention had been fixed at the time on the actual words rather than the accent, but now that he thought about it, there had been something . . .

Jane was talking about Beryl. 'If she can't get here, then we're cut off till the snow melts. Alone in the frozen wastes. Pity we haven't got a string of huskies, or skis, or anything useful.'

'Rubbish!' Isobel sounded scornful. 'Beryl gives up easily. It's only a few inches of snow, and it can't be more than half a mile to her house.'

'Our nearest neighbour,' Jane sighed. 'How's the food supply? We'd better ration the water. And the coke.'

'No problem,' Isobel said acidly, 'so long as Ben forgets to wash his hands before meals.'

Ben took no notice. He kept the peace by gathering up all the plates and heaving them into the sink. He stood for some time looking out of the window at the patterns made by the kitchen light on the smooth snow outside, before he eventually turned on the tap and reached for the bottle of washing-up liquid. Isobel glanced at him in surprise, but made no comment. She and Jane went to watch the television, and it was half an hour before Ben joined them.

As soon as he appeared, Isobel decided it was time to turn it off. Ben was neither annoyed nor surprised. There was a frown on his face, and he said good-night absent-mindedly. He listened to them banging about upstairs, heard the sound of Isobel's radio, waited. The last thing Isobel had said was to turn off the light and see that the fire was safe and the doors locked.

For the last ten minutes Ben had been sitting in the dark with only the last embers of the fire to throw a red glow across the carpet. He fixed the guard, stood up, stretched, went out to the hall to fetch his old coat and his red scarf, then quietly crept to the back door. It didn't squeak as he eased it open. He stood on the step watching the strange radiance which gleamed on the surface of the frozen snow, and the dark shadows beyond, where a little wood separated the garden from the meadows which ran down to the stream. It was cold, without a breath of wind, but at least it had stopped snowing.

Ben turned his gaze in the direction of Cole's Hill. If he expected to see any glow of light from the shepherd's hut, he was disappointed. The ancient earth ramparts which surrounded the top hid it from view. There was no moon, just that faint lustre on the snow, enough to show him what he had thought he had seen from the kitchen window. At the time he had decided to say nothing about it, but now it was as clear as day. A line of footprints coming from the wood, across the garden, up to the kitchen window; and another line intermingled with it as the maker of the footprints had gone.

Quietly Ben closed the door behind him and stepped into the night.

## *Chapter Three*

It was easy to follow the line of disturbed snow across the garden and into the shadows of the trees. When Ben reached the meadow beyond, he stopped for a moment and watched the silent white expanse lit by the moon. Unless they had all been stepping in the same prints, only one man had come to the kitchen window and gone away again. Ben thought he knew why. The men at the shepherd's hut had captured his anorak, and inside it, clearly printed, was his name and address. They'd wanted to check the truth of it, see how the land lay, make a guess at the enemy strength. Well, they knew that now. Two girls and a boy. Nobody else. And the house half a mile from the nearest neighbour, and the roads full of snow. They weren't to know that the only grown-up in the house was away for two days, but all the same it must look to them like a marvellous piece of luck.

Somehow Ben had to steer them away from the house. It occurred to him as he looked over the meadow and the stream beyond, that he ought to tell the local police. But it seemed tame, somehow. He'd keep that possibility in reserve.

The line of footprints marched straight across to the hedge where Ben knew a gate led into the lane. Nothing stirred in the glistening snow, except for a solitary night bird that swooped and circled in complete silence and then disappeared into the trees. Ben pulled his scarf round his head, stuffed his hands into his pockets, and followed the line, trying to match his steps with the holes already made.

The gate was stuck fast in a drift, but he could see where the man had climbed over and dislodged the icing of snow from the top bar. Ben tried a gate-vault, a thing he could normally do with ease, but his hands slipped on the cold wood and he landed in an untidy heap in the ditch at the side of the lane. Like a dog he shook himself free of snow. The lines of prints followed the ditch, making straight for Cole's Hill.

Ben stopped and considered. So far he had been right. The most likely thing was that one of the men from the shephed's hut had come down to investigate, been satisfied, had gone back. So what should he do now? And, more important, what would the men do? They had found out where he lived—

Ben's thoughts came to a sudden stop. All right, so his address had been in the anorak. *He* knew where it was, of course. But how did *they* know enough to come straight there? Two possibilities came into Ben's head. Either they were local people, though he had not recognized them and they hadn't sounded local, or they had got their information from someone else. But who would have been out and about on a night like this?

Ben began to trudge along the lane with his head still buzzing with the problem. He was making for Cole's Hill, but in these conditions it would take him half an hour to reach the woods which lay around its base. He had walked for ten minutes when he was brought up short by a low soft chuckle from the hedge.

Ben dived for the ditch, his scalp tingling and his breath held inside his chest until he thought his lungs would burst. A flurry of snow flew round him, settled on his face.

Again the soft chuckle.

Ben pulled himself out of the ditch. He was annoyed with himself. He told himself he should have known. He was passing Laxton wood, and in the middle of it was an old decrepit barn, one of St Michael's favourite haunts.

An old and wrinkled and hairy face peered at him over the top of a broken gate. St Michael was a harmless old tramp who walked all day and refused to be taken care of by those

whom he called interfering busybodies.

'By the holy Michael and all his angels,' the old man said between his chuckles, 'but you came a beautiful cropper.'

'Evening,' Ben said, trying to forget his panic.

'And a late one to be out in. Me, I don't sleep. 'Tis cold weather for a snooze.'

'Seen anyone around tonight, St Michael?'

'Not a soul. Barring yourself, and a stray fox on the prowl. You ought to be home.'

Ben brushed the suggestion aside. If St Michael had been there all evening, and he didn't miss much, he must have seen the man from Cole's Hill, and, if he had, why didn't he say so?

Something that Jane had said earlier suddenly came back to him. Irish accents. The IRA. Explosions. And here was a man with the most obvious Irish accent this side of Dublin Town. Ben looked at St Michael with abrupt suspicion. Somebody must have told the man from Cole's Hill the way to come, but surely not St Michael? He always knew what was going on, but he usually kept it to himself.

'Sure you've seen no one?'

'There may have been an odd man . . .'

'How odd?'

St Michael's only reply was another quiet chuckle. Then he flapped the sleeves of his long coat, whirled round, and disappeared into the wood.

'And the same to you,' Ben remarked to nobody. He wondered what to do next. He *had* been on his way to Cole's Hill, though he had no definite plan in mind. Now that he had seen old St Michael, and had been reminded of Irish accents, he was even less sure. He pulled the scarf tighter round his neck, hoping that it would make up for the ragged holes in his old anorak, and ploughed on.

There were a few fine flakes of snow in the air now, not enough to stop him seeing his way ahead, and certainly not enough to make him turn back, but they emphasised the cold and the difficulty of pushing one leg after another through the drifts. When he came to the dark belt of trees at the foot of the hill, he paused for breath. Now that he had come so far, there was no alternative but to continue.

It was dark beneath the snow-laden branches, and the clumps of bramble and dead grass caught at his feet and his clothes. What was he trying to do, anyway? Find enough information to convince Isobel and Jane, he supposed, not that they would ever believe anything he said. Still, it would be good to have something definite to present to them in the morning, especially if it was a stick of dynamite . . .

Abruptly he was out of the woods, and the hill stretched away before him like a great white tablecloth, fringed by the first of the earth ramparts. The lines of footprints, one set down and the other up, stood out like arrows beckoning him on his way, beginning now to be obscured by the fresh snow but still distinct. Manfully he set himself to the stiff climb.

As his head came level with the top of the rampart, he waited, expecting danger. But nothing came to his gaze except whiteness and the track he was following. He was surprised how far he could see, now that the wind had cleared the mist. When he reached the top of the second rampart, the whole level surface of the hill lay before him, quiet and peaceful and strangely safe.

At first he could not see the hut. He had expected a blaze of light, or at least a gleam from the ill-fitting boards which formed the walls. But there was nothing to guide him except those everlasting footprints. Not that they *would* last for ever, he thought: the few odd flakes were already beginning to smudge the outlines. By morning there'd be nothing left.

Quietly and cautiously he followed the line, his eyes alert for any sign of movement ahead, and then, suddenly, there was the hut, just over a ridge in the land, lying squat and black against the snow.

But no light, no sound, no sign of life.

Ben felt a temptation struggling in his chest to yell and to shout, even to sing, to dare them to come out after him, so that at least he would know where they were. His muscles tensed as he fought against the temptation. He might be a fool – Isobel was always telling him so – but he wasn't as silly as that.

He crept along the side of the hut, looked for the knot-hole, found it with his fingers, applied one eye, saw nothing. Curious, he turned the corner to the front where the door rested on rusty hinges. It was half-open.

What *was* this? Some sort of trap?

With sudden fear he whipped his head round, expecting to find three bulky figures surrounding him, arms raised, faces split in monstrous grins. His foot slipped in the snow and he fell, his head hitting the door with a sound like a gun, his fingers scrabbling at the door-step.

He lay for a moment, the breath forced out of his lungs and his legs refusing to move. This, he thought, was where he found out just how stupid he'd been . . .

But nothing happened.

Carefully he pulled himself up, dusted the loose snow off

his jeans, pushed the door wider. A grin spread across his face. He needn't have bothered, after all. Nobody at home.

He stepped inside, keeping the door open with one hand so that the dim radiance of the snow showed him the boarded floor, and something small and dark lying in one corner. Gingerly he stirred it with a foot. It was soft, yielding, and oddly familiar.

His grin widened. Nice of them to leave his anorak behind when they cleared out. They'd gone, probably for good. Frightened because they'd been discovered. They realized they'd been overheard, so they'd gone to find another hiding-place.

A pity, really, Ben reflected. He would have liked to know what they'd been up to, and now he never would. He picked up his anorak, bundled it into a ball, pushed it under one arm.

Outside, he peered at the snow. In front of the door it was disturbed, close-packed, dirty. Across the top of the hill three lines of footprints marched away.

'Well, that proves it,' Ben said aloud. 'Footprints going away, and none coming back. This snow has its uses, after all.' He stood gazing out across the white desert. 'The village is over there,' he muttered. 'Must be all of two miles over the top and into the valley. Well, they can go by themselves. I've had enough.'

He was pleased with himself, though he had no one to share his satisfaction with. Certainly, he wouldn't bother to tell Isobel just how he had recovered his anorak. 'Found it lying about,' he'd say, and she'd believe him. With luck.

He was whistling quietly as he came to the ramparts. A final glance over his shoulder to reassure himself, then he was running down the steep slope, having to run in order to keep up with his feet, until he reached the sombre shadows of the trees. He'd have to go carefully here: the woods were full of traps for the unwary.

There was no sign of old St Michael along the lane. Ben

had a picture of him, tucked up in plenty of newspaper in a corner of the barn set back from the road. He was safe enough. St Michael always said that the angels looked after their own.

Ben slipped into a copse at the bottom of the garden, stopped for a moment to see if anyone was waiting for him. Isobel with a frying-pan, he thought, but there was no light in any of the windows. Quite right, too. Even he was prepared to admit that he could use some sleep . . .

The back door resisted his pressure, and he pushed it harder. Something to do with the weather, he supposed. The wood was sticking, perhaps frozen.

Gradually the truth dawned in his head. Some idiot had pushed the bolt across.

# Chapter Four

Ben went all round the house looking for an open window, but his luck was out. He himself, earlier in the day, had removed the spare backdoor key from its usual hiding-place below the sill of the kitchen window – for safety's sake, he had said efficiently, and now he cursed himself for it.

He stood at the back door, wondering whether a good swift kick might do the trick, but he knew that any noise would bring Isobel down on him at once, full of questions and complaints and needless worries, and it would all be stored up in her elephant's brain for future use.

It was as he pondered the wisdom of throwing snowballs at an upstairs window, that the squeak of wood came to his frozen ears. He looked up. Not Isobel, but Jane. Her round face, circled by long dark hair, peered at him.

'If it's Father Christmas,' she said, like a grand lady receiving the call of a vacuum cleaner salesman, 'tell him he's a week early. The tradesmen's entrance is at the rear.'

Ben was not prepared to put up with this sort of thing. 'Come on down and open this blasted door,' he muttered. Any moment Isobel would wake up and want to know.

'The reindeer are eating the Brussels sprouts,' Jane said crushingly, 'and otherwise misbehaving themselves. Book tokens will be gratefully received.'

'All right, all *right*! Just open up, will you?'

'Haven't you got a key?'

'Course I haven't. If I had, I wouldn't be standing here with my teeth falling out with the cold, would I? The door's bolted.'

'That will be Isobel.'

Ben groaned. 'You won't tell her?'

'Depends what it's worth.' A faint giggle floated down through the frosty air. 'Oh, Ben, you do look funny. Like a snowman that's seen trouble. I'll be down in a minute.'

The minute passed slowly while Ben kicked his feet into the snow and tried to keep warm. Eventually metal slithered and wood creaked.

'How nice of you to come,' Jane said. She had wrapped herself in an old dressing-gown, and she was laughing.

Ben ignored the laugh. He pushed past her and made for the switch of the electric fire. 'Is Bel awake?'

'Not yet. But she'll want to know why there's a damp patch just there in the morning. Ben, you could have left all that snow outside.'

Ben only growled.

'I'll make some tea,' Jane offered, 'and there's some biscuits left in that tin. Isobel won't miss half a dozen.'

'Yes, she will,' Ben said. Not that he cared. 'I went out to get my anorak,' he explained. 'I got it, too.'

'Clever. Where was it?'

'Up on the hill,' Ben said vaguely. Jane was busy with the kettle and she seemed satisfied with his answer. Ben threw his anorak on to a chair and stretched his hands to the fire. The tea, when it came, was hot, and after a few minutes he began to feel better.

'Were they still there?' Jane asked innocently.

'No. Not a trace. Except for the marks of their feet. They must have gone over the hill and down to the village.'

'Shows sense, in this weather. No explosions?'

'Not yet.'

'Well, we'll just have to wait and see. Tell Father Christmas he can call again.' Jane left him to the fire. Ben sat for a few minutes more, thinking. At length he came to the conclusion that there was nothing he could do, so the adventure was over. Not much of an adventure, really. Just as well Isobel's room was at the front of the house. With luck, she'd never know.

Ben slept late. It was Jane who eventually woke him up by standing at the end of his bed and throwing socks at him. 'Trouble,' she said mysteriously. 'Plenty of it. I'd advise a quick sneak out of the window before she catches you.'

Ben groaned. 'You've told her.'

'Not me. Didn't have to. I'll keep her in the kitchen while you escape, if you like.'

'But I haven't had any breakfast.'

'There's more important things than coffee and rice crispies. Isobel is on the warpath. Don't say you weren't warned.'

'Thanks,' Ben said.

'Don't mention it. What are sisters for?'

'I've often wondered.'

Ben took a long time washing and dressing, but hunger at last drove him down. Isobel was at the kitchen table, rolling out something that looked like grey pastry. So, Ben thought, she was armed. He slid into a chair at the table and tried to look invisible. Isobel didn't say a word, and that, he knew, was always a bad sign. Jane was curled up in a chair by the fire, pretending to read. Outside the window, the snow lay thick, fresh, and undisturbed. There was a bright blue sky and icicles were beginning to form on the gutter of the shed.

Ben wished rice crispies didn't make so much noise. He gulped hot coffee, reached for his anorak, made for the door.

'Just a minute,' Isobel said, like the schoolmistress she would probably become.

'Busy,' Ben said.

'No, you're not. Where did this come from?' She produced a page torn from a magazine and slapped it down on the table in front of him.

Ben stared, then laughed. 'You're not old enough, Bel,' he told her. The page had come from one of those magazines that newsagents keep on the top shelf, and the colours were crude and blatant.

'Your new anorak was on that chair this morning,' Isobel

said remorselessly. 'I picked it up and this fell out. Well?'

Ben was thinking furiously, but Jane interrupted. 'Tell her, Ben, it's the only clean way. She might even believe you.'

Ben muttered and grumbled, but eventually he told her. In any case, Bel had a way of finding things out, so she'd be sure to know sooner or later. She listened to him with a frown on her face and her hands busy with the pastry. When he finished, she said 'You could have told me. At least I ought to know where you are.'

For Bel, that was mild. 'Sorry,' Ben mumbled.

'I thought you'd started smoking as well.'

'Oh?' Ben had once found a packet of cigarettes by the stream, had taken them to the old mill for a quiet experiment, and after three puffs had thrown the rest in the water. He hoped Bel didn't know about that.

'French ones, too.' She tossed a crumpled packet on the table. 'This was with that magazine.'

Ben straightened out the packet, but there was nothing in it. Jane uncurled from the chair and came over to have a look.

'Somebody's been doodling,' she said, pointing to the picture on the front of the packet. 'Green biro, unless my eyes deceive me.'

'So what?' Ben was bored with the whole business. 'I'll be back about midday.'

Isobel barred his way to the door. 'We're going into the village. Lots of things we need, especially if the snow lasts.'

'You can always phone old Mother Murphy at the shop.'

'I've tried. The line must be down. The weight of the snow or something.'

Ben knew what was coming. He'd be expected to trail round behind Isobel while she had all the fun of picking and choosing, and then he'd have to carry the bags.

'We're all going,' Isobel said firmly. 'And, Ben, you can carry the bags.'

Silly old wart-hog, Ben thought, but he kept it to himself.

It was hard work ploughing through the few inches of snow along the lane. The small amount which had fallen during the night had softened the edges of the footprints which Ben had followed the previous evening, and the only new marks were the wheel-treads of the milk-float, and the little arrowheads of a bird's feet. But at least the sun was shining, though it produced no great heat. It was their own exertions which kept them warm.

There was quite a crowd in the village shop. Everybody seemed to have had the same idea of stocking up for bad weather. Ben fidgeted while they waited. The trouble with the village shop was that everybody who came there wanted to gossip. It was some years since so much snow had fallen before Christmas, and most people had their own tales to tell of burst pipes and frozen milk and rotting cabbages.

Ben's mind wandered. That packet of cigarettes which he'd bundled up with his anorak in the shepherd's hut might have been bought at this very shop, though he didn't suppose that anyone would remember its sale. The lurid magazine which had shocked Isobel, though – now, that was a different matter. Only one place in the village would have sold that, the newsagent's down the street.

Ben edged to the door and slipped through. Isobel was busy picking out packets of biscuits and didn't notice him go. He ran to the newsagent's, went in, glanced along the racks of magazines. There they all were, up on the top shelf, out of his reach. Not that he had enough money to buy that sort of stuff, anyway. He picked up a copy of the Beano, searched in his pocket for the necessary coins, and said to the youth behind the corner 'You can't beat the oldies, Alf.'

Alf was prepared to unbend since there were no other customers. Ben had known him for a long time, though never well. He was tall, thin, and gloomy.

'Ta,' he said, taking the money.

'You don't look busy,' Ben offered.

'Not this time of day. All the work gets done early in this game. If you want that bar of chocolate, it'll cost you.'

Ben kept his fingers to himself. 'Much call for that stuff up there?' He nodded in the direction of the top shelf.

'You'd be surprised. Bit young, aren't you? Mind you, some very rum folk come in for that.'

'Like who?'

'Old Mrs Grace, for one.'

Ben looked suitably impressed. 'Go on!'

'Sure thing. Said she wanted it for her gardener, but they all say that.'

'Anyone else?'

'What do you what to know for?'

'Just curious.'

'Not that I can think of.'

'Two tall fellows, and a little short fat one?'

'That's funny, you saying that. There was a group of them, laughing and joking. I kept my eyes open, 'cos I thought they was going to walk off without paying.'

'When was that?'

'Two days ago, something like that. Friends of yours?'

'Not exactly.'

'Funny if they was, 'cos one of 'em's just crossing the road right this minute. Coming this way, too.'

# *Chapter Five*

Ben dived for the cover of the counter. Alf backed away, as though afraid he was going to be attacked. He put up a hand to protect his face, but Ben was interested only in the glass door leading to the street. His eyes peered through a display of peppermints. Alf had been right: it was the short fat one and his hand was already on the door knob. Ben ducked down.

'Hey!' Alf exclaimed. His mouth gaped open, and he seemed incapable of further speech. And that, Ben considered, was just as well.

'*Twenty gitanes.*'

Ben hugged the back of the counter. Just as well the thing was solid rather than glass, but he would have liked to get a better look at the man who was asking for French cigarettes. He sounded more American, though, than Irish.

'Wake up, boy. Twenty gitanes, I said.'

'Sir.'

Ben was aware of Alf moving above him, of Alf's feet dangerously near his head. He shifted slightly, dislodged a stack of magazines from an under-counter shelf. Alf stooped. His horrified eyes met Ben's.

'You do your tidying up after I've gone,' the short fat man told him. 'Look slippy with those cigs. Who was that boy in here?'

'Boy?' Alf said, straightening his back and looking stupid.

'Yeah. They're the ones that's different from girls. Who was he?'

'Boy?' Alf said again.

The short fat man gave it up in disgust. Muttering something about village idiots, he paid for the cigarettes and went. Ben watched him round the edge of the counter. Dark jeans, red woodman's shirt, dirty anorak, porkpie hat. And an American accent. Not that it helped much.

The man turned to shut the door, and as he did so, his eyes met Ben's. Ben dodged back. The man let out a yell and charged back in. There was nothing Ben could do but retreat, and in the process Alf had to be sacrificed. He grabbed Alf's ankles, pulled; brought him crashing down like a felled tree. Alf's arms swept the counter clear of papers, peppermints, and chewing gum, and the whole lot fell on top of him as he lay sprawled on the floor. The man skidded to a halt and Ben dived for the door at the back. He had no idea where it led, but that didn't seem to matter much. He slammed the door shut behind him, put his back against it, found a key in the lock, turned it. Just in time. the door shook as the man in the shop attacked it with fists and feet.

Ben's brain was racing. Why had the man been so keen to get hold of him? Surely it would have been better for the three on Cole's Hill, whatever their little plot, to keep out of trouble and out of sight? And here they were, or at least one of them, making themselves obvious. Poor old Alf would be on to the police as soon as he got that chewing gum out of his hair. Not that that would do him much good: the nearest police station was five miles away.

Meanwhile Ben had to get out. There was nobody in the little back store-room, and only one small window high up in the opposite wall, but there was a door. Ben pulled it open. The lock was a yale, so there was nothing he could do but close it behind him. The noise of the man's attack was muffled now, and in a couple of seconds it stopped.

Ben looked round. He was in a back yard stacked with boxes, crates, and cartons, and surrounded by a high fence. The gate in the fence was locked. Ben swore softly.

It took him a moment or two to assemble enough crates to build up a rickety platform. He wished he could still hear the man's hammering: at least, then he would know where he was. Silence meant he might have realized he could work his way round the back of the shop and cut off Ben's escape.

Ben scrambled up to the top of the fence, put one leg over, sat for a moment watching, then let himself drop to the worn grass below. The light covering of snow helped to break his fall. He picked himself up and was at once ready to run. A long thin lane, with high fences on both sides, and a building at the far end. He'd be caught like a rat in a drainpipe, if the man appeared at the other end. Ben ran.

The lane came out into a side-road off the village's main street. Ben put his head cautiously round the corner, but there was no sign of the man who smoked French cigarettes. Ben's shoulders relaxed. He felt pleased with himself. He thought he had dealt with the emergency in convincingly heroic style. Pity about Alf. Still, he'd recover. The only fly in the ointment was that, with all the confusion, Ben realized he'd left his Beano behind. He didn't feel much like going back to rescue it.

He started walking to the main street.

'Hey, Ben!'

Ben spun round, his fists up and ready, then he relaxed. It was Jane.

'Ben, where have you *been*?'

'Here and there.'

'Well, never mind that now. Isobel is still in the shop, buying enough for a siege, I should think. I said I'd meet her outside when she'd finished.'

Ben groaned. He didn't like the sound of this. It had already been made clear to him that he would be expected to do the carrying. They ought to have brought the sledge. Except that it broke last year, and Ben hadn't yet got round to mending it.

'Ben, I had an idea.'

'Oh?' Ben didn't sound convinced.

Jane's serious face broke into a grin. 'I do, sometimes. I

was thinking about what you said last night, about the explosions and the blowing-up of someone important.'

Ben was surprised. He hadn't really thought that Jane had either taken much notice or even believed him. 'Well?'

'It would help if we knew who's going to be blown up, wouldn't it?'

'Sure, but—'

'So we find out. Come on.'

Jane began to drag him into a nearby building. When he was inside, Ben realized that it was the little local library. Trust Jane to know that. She spent most of her time in this poky little place.

'They always keep copies of the local Gazette,' Jane said. 'Over here.'

Ben turned the pages while Jane muttered to herself. Nobody took any notice of them. Three women were gossiping in a corner, and the librarian was busy putting books back on the shelves.

'What are we looking for?' Ben wanted to know.

'Shush!' Jane told him, and went on muttering. 'Councillors, petty theft at the butcher's, new sewage works, special carol service at St Aldate's, more Councillors, row over burning garden rubbish – that'll be the Council again – football results, small ads, that's the lot.'

'Well?' Ben asked. 'No Queen, no Prime Minister, not even a tin-pot general?'

'Nope.' Jane looked at the wall opposite with evident annoyance. 'There *must* be some reason for what you heard, Ben. Unless you were making it all up.'

'I didn't. And I wasn't making up that thug in the paper-shop five minutes ago.'

'What thug? Alf's all right when you get to know him.'

Ben realized he had made a mistake. Tell Jane half a story and she always wanted to know the rest. 'We'd better go and find Bel,' he suggested.

'Not until you've told me about the thug.'

'Oh, come on!' Ben said, exasperated.

The librarian looked at them severely. Jane glared back, but she knew when she was beaten. Reluctantly she allowed Ben to drag her out, but only as far as the street.

'If I'm going to keep Isobel off your back,' she said, 'I've got to know the facts.'

Ben told her. 'The trouble is,' he finished, 'he saw me. Knows what I look like.' He glanced along the street, but there was no sign of the short man who smoked French cigarettes. They walked to the village shop.

'Look at her!' Ben exclaimed, pointing through the window at Isobel. 'She's still at it.'

'It keeps her quiet,' Jane commented. She looked along the length of the village street. Plenty of black timbers, higgledy-piggledy roofs, leaning chimneys, olde English windows – but no thugs. 'The thing is, Ben, we don't know what they're intending to *do*.'

'If we did, it'd be easy to stop them. Well, fairly easy.'

Jane giggled. 'The post-mistress? The vicar? There's his name over there on the notice-board.' Jane crossed the road to the stone church with the tall spire and neglected graveyard. 'Rev Gerard Smythe, that's who he is.' She contemplated a great red poster which hung from the notice-board. '6.30 Evensong with traditional carols. Blessing by the Bishop of Stanton. Who's he?'

Ben shrugged. 'Don't ask me.' He was feeling depressed. He didn't know what to do, and he resented Jane's interference. 'St Aldate's isn't worth blowing up,' he said morosely. He didn't sing in tune himself, and though he knew a number of boys who sang in St Aldate's choir, he had no wish to join them. 'It's all clean cassocks and straighten your tie,' he observed.

'What?'

'St Aldate's. Anyway, the Bishop can look after himself.' He stopped suddenly and glanced again at the notice-board. An idea was beginning to grow in his mind, and he was trying to work out whether it was believable, or just plain silly. He looked at the church with new interest. It was a grey building, covered in ivy and moss, with a tall spire not quite straight, and pointed windows. A gate in the churchyard wall led through a forest of tipsy gravestones to a porch.

Ben acted on impulse. He was pushing open the heavy old door inside the porch before Jane could stop him.

'You're not allowed,' she objected.

'Course I am. Anyone is. Anyway, there's nobody to stop me.'

Inside, the church smelt of mice, hymn-books, and forgotten generations of choir-boys. It was dim, quiet, almost ghostly. Ben tip-toed up to the chancel where the choir stalls faced each other across a black and white patterned stone floor. Boughs of holly hung from the beams, and somebody had put a spray of mistletoe over the pulpit. Presumably, Ben thought, it was a joke. He was surprised, but not particularly interested. He stood on the steps between the choir-stalls and looked back over the length of the nave with its squat plain columns and rows of dark pews. He raised an arm, pretending to be the Bishop blessing the flock, and Jane giggled. The light came through the stained-glass windows and made patterns on the stone floor. Ben began to enjoy himself.

Suddenly Jane stopped laughing. 'Somebody's coming,' she whispered, almost afraid.

'So what? We're not doing anything wrong.'

The great oak door in the porch opened wide, and a voice said 'This is the place, Jed, so you can stop smoking right now.' It was an American voice, one that Ben instantly recognised.

# *Chapter Six*

Ben sprang to the back of the pulpit, hoping that Jane would have sufficient sense to follow him without being told. She was by his side almost at once, but her sense did not make her keep quiet. She was tugging at Ben's arm and trying to whisper to him, but all Ben's attention was fixed on the porch.

'Cosy little place for the carols,' the American voice said.

Ben peered through the holes in a carving of the infant Samuel. It was the second time in an hour that he had seen this short fat man, and on both occasions he'd been hiding. He was getting used to it. They might just as well, he thought, be playing some sort of kids' game of Chase Me.

He tried to see the man to whom short fatty was talking. There he was, the tall one who had chased him on Cole's Hill.

'His nibs won't be hearing the carols,' the tall man said.

Ben was sure now. An Irish accent – not that this fact seemed to be of much use at the moment. He squeezed his face past the infant Samuel, trying to see more, and all the time Jane was pulling at him. Irritably he shook her off.

'Quiet in here, Jed, quiet as the grave.' A little spurt of laughter, instantly checked.

Too right, Ben reflected, far too quiet. They could probably hear his heart thumping inside his chest. Jane's fingers made little scratching noises on his anorak, like industrious mice. He glanced over his shoulder for a way of escape. Nothing but brown pews and coloured patterns on the floor. There was a big door up by the side of the altar, but he'd be sure to be seen if he tried to cross the red carpet between that and the chancel steps. Another door, tucked away behind the pulpit, its great iron latch fast in its socket. Ben put out a hand and applied pressure to the handle. Nothing. He'd need a battering ram to shift it.

'Haven't you seen enough, Jed? Come on, let's get out of here. What's the interest, anyway? You gone religious?'

'Used to be a choir-boy once.' The second voice was nearer now, more distinct, menacing. 'Read the lessons, too.'

'Go on!' A great burst of laughter sprang from the short fat man. Ben seized his chance. He put his weight against the door, and it moved with a squeal and a shriek.

'What's that?'

'Sarcastic laughter.'

'Something else.'

'It's the ghosts gibbering. You'll hear them playing the bones soon.' Another burst of harsh laughter.

Ben slipped through and pulled Jane behind him. He didn't dare close the door after them, afraid of the squealing hinges, and in any case it was dark in the narrow little passage. A flight of worn stone steps curved up into the blackness above his head.

'Come on!' he whispered, hoping that the ghosts kept to ground level.

Their feet fell softly in the thick dust on the stairs. They climbed up and up, round and round, making for a spot of light above their heads. A tiny window set in the massive tower wall pointed their way, like a star, but beyond it was darkness even deeper.

Ben's legs were beginning to ache. He could not go back, not yet, so there was no choice but to continue up. Surely no church tower could be this high? He'd be needing oxygen soon.

At length they came to the top of the stairs where another solid door barred their way. Ben gave it a push, and it swung open with hardly a murmur. Typical, he reflected, now that they no longer needed to be quiet. No sound of pursuit had come to him from below.

They stepped out into a narrow walk which stretched all the way round the tower. On one side was a parapet, like a castle's battlements, stopping them falling over the edge, and in the middle rose the enormous finger of the spire.

Jane was leaning over the battlements. 'Ooh, look,' she said. 'There's Isobel.'

Ben glanced over. 'So it is. She's cross, too. You can tell by the way she's kicking that old tincan in the gutter. Temper.'

'Do you think she'd hear us?'

'Not a chance,' Ben said firmly. 'But those two down below would.'

'What do we do, then?' Jane looked at him with a trusting expression which Ben didn't often see.

'Wait. A few minutes, anyway. With luck, Bel will give it up and cart that lot of shopping home by herself.'

'She won't. It's cold up here, Ben.' Jane dragged her fingers along the parapet and made a firm snowball. 'Could you hit her from here?'

The possibility intrigued Ben. It was a question of range as well as angle. He narrowed his eyes in an effort of appraisal. 'You'd probably kill her if you dropped it on her head,' he said at length, regretfully.

'Oh, well. Have we waited long enough?'

Ben went back to the door. The stair-well acted like a funnel, and he thought he could hear movement and voices from down below. 'Shush!' he muttered.

He was right. Thin ghostly voices, like a breath of air in the tree tops, came to his straining ears. Somebody was talking, but it wasn't either the American or the Irishman. Very English, high, penetrating. Probably the vicar, he thought.

'What if they lock that door?' Jane whispered. She sounded almost scared.

'Then we start chucking snow at Isobel, whether it kills her or not,' Ben grumbled. 'Shut up!'

'*Some early English work, though mainly perpendicular.*'

'*Gee! Fancy that.*'

'*Would you like to see the tower?*'

(Blast the vicar, Ben thought irreverently. What did he want to come barging in for?)

'*Some other time, say?*'

'*As you wish. The church is always open.*'

'*A bit risky, isn't it?*'

'*So people say. But so far nothing has been stolen from the church. My vicarage, now, that's another matter. Burglars only the other night. Not that there is much to take, of course, and I think I must have disturbed them when I came back from the Committee in Aid of the Depressed. We call it Cad's, for short. A joke, you know.*'

The vicar's chuckle floated up the stair-well, like a leaf caught in the breeze.

Ben decided he'd had enough of waiting about in a howling gale on a church tower. He was still worried by the thought that the vicar might lock the door at the bottom of the stone stairs. Carefully he began the long descent. Jane looked anxious, but at least she didn't say anything.

It seemed like hours before they reached the foot of the stairs and stood in the shadow of the door peering through the narrow gap. All they could see was a round jolly little man with glasses and his collar back to front. He was lecturing his unseen audience about church architecture, and it sounded as though he could go on for an hour or two yet. Ben grinned to himself in the darkness. That would keep those two thugs nicely occupied, while he and Jane crept out and tried for a dramatic escape. It depended, of course, just where the thugs were, and whether the main door was open. Ben slipped round the edge of the door and took up his familiar position by the infant Samuel. He did

not have long to wait, as the vicar's audience was growing restive. A few more rounded sentences, and the Rev Gerard Smythe was talking to himself.

Ben emerged, trying to look as though he was interested in stone carvings or pew-ends or even brass rubbings. He attempted a familiar nod at the vicar as he passed.

'Good gracious!' the vicar exclaimed, surprised. 'Ye gods and little fishes! Where have you two sprung from?'

'We were inspecting the tower,' Jane said, deciding that honesty was the only policy in the presence of the clergy. 'Very interesting.'

'You think so? A late fifteenth century addition, I am afraid. Have you been up to the top? You must be tired. Come and have an orange juice or a hot chocolate. I am sure Mrs Smythe will be delighted.'

Ben wasn't keen, but for some reason Jane wanted to go. As the vicar led the way, she hissed at Ben 'He said he'd been burgled a few days ago. It must mean something.'

'Oh?' Ben said, perplexed. He was thinking of Isobel kicking snow at the front of the village shop, but he didn't have much alternative.

The vicar's wife was less welcoming than the vicar had supposed, but she brought them glasses of orange and a plate of plain biscuits. 'I'm always prepared,' she remarked acidly, 'for any stray waifs the vicar brings home.'

'Did you have much stolen?' Jane asked directly.

'The burglars? No. The vicar's diary, and a bottle of sherry.'

'His diary?' Ben repeated.

The vicar looked put out. 'My dear, our young friends hardly want to know our small losses and discomforts. If it had been only the sherry, I might have suspected that tramp who wanders the hedge-rows.'

'St Michael?'

'I believe he is known by that appellation. Not entirely respectfully, I venture to think. As I said, the sherry might point to – er – St Michael, but I cannot imagine what use he could find for the diary of my engagements.'

Jane was wandering. She seemed to be interested in the litter which covered the vicar's desk. 'Do you always use green ink?' she asked suddenly.

'Why, as a matter of actual fact, I do. Have you discovered one of my green biros? I find that green is restful to the eyes.' The vicar beamed.

'And you smoke,' Jane went on, like counsel for the prosecution.

'Well, yes, I must confess—'

'I thought you must. There's a packet here, those French ones. And you've been scribbling on the front.'

'A habit of mine. Doodling, you know. Oh, must you go? Do drop in again, and if you are at all interested in church architecture—'

Somehow Ben found himself outside.

'Phew!' he exploded. 'Jane, you ought to be on a funny farm. So should he. Whatever made you get involved with him?'

'A burglary' Jane said. Her dark eyes were shining.

'We'd better go and find Bel,' Ben urged. Sometimes he found his sister too much of a handful. 'She'll be tearing her hair out.'

'That won't hurt her. Ben, think! Somebody broke into the vicarage, pinched a bottle of sherry, and a diary. And probably a packet of cigarettes as well, French ones, doodled all over with green biro.'

'Like the one wrapped up in my anorak.'

'Course.'

'Do you think that magazine came from the vicar as well?'

Jane giggled. 'You never can tell. Well, anyway, somebody stole his cigarettes, liked them, and bought some more and took them up to the shepherd's hut. You know that from Alf at the newsagent's.'

'So?'

'Either the vicar is involved with your thugs, and not even you could believe that, or they wanted something more important than sherry and cigarettes.'

'The old boy's diary.'

'What else?'

Ben frowned, but he had no time to consider the suggestion.

'*Ben*!' a shrill voice yelled at him. 'Where have you *been*?'

## *Chapter Seven*

The walk back through the white snow-bound landscape was a silent affair. Isobel was plainly furious, and said so whenever she had the chance. Jane was amused. Ben needed all his breath for lugging the plastic bags full of the things Isobel had bought. He found it was easier to drag them over the hard slippery surface, until one of them hit a sharp stone and burst, scattering its contents over a wide area. The incident did not improve Isobel's temper.

'You'll just have to use your hands,' she told him without sympathy.

'You and Jane could take a few more,' Ben suggested.

'No.'

Ben stripped off his anorak, bundled everything inside and tied it up with the sleeves. He then searched the hedge for a stick, and having found one, hoisted the whole lot on to his shoulder. After that, he began to enjoy himself. They were nearly home when the sleeves came undone, but by that time it no longer mattered.

The lane, Ben noted, was still untrodden by anyone except themselves.

Isobel usually liked to do the cooking herself. She was good at it, and the other two were happy to let her get on with it, but on this occasion Ben thought he'd better help. By the time he had scraped the potatoes to a size something like marbles, allowed one saucepan to boil over, and broken a cup, he was beginning to wonder whether it was such a good idea. Jane was curled up in her usual chair with a book, and took no notice of either of them. But that was normal, too.

When Isobel was nearly ready with the food, Jane

uncurled herself and put the knives and forks out, like one looking down from a great height to help the starving poor. Ben raised his eyebrows, but decided not to comment.

'The diary,' Jane said suddenly.

'The vicar's?'

'That very one. Significant, don't you agree, Ben?'

Isobel broke in. 'What are you two chattering about?'

Jane told her what had happened in the church. 'We couldn't tell you before,' she finished, 'not in the mood you were in.'

Isobel banged a saucepan. 'I am *not* in a temper.'

'Course not. It's just that – oh, well, there it is. The vicar's diary was pinched, together with his secret supply of sherry and his cigs. It'll do him good to go without.'

'Odd, that,' Ben said. 'The green biro, and everything. There's got to be a connection. No ordinary burglar would bother about a vicarage, but those three thugs up on the hill did, and instead of pinching the telly, they walk off with his diary. Why?'

'Because,' Isobel said, almost cheerfully, 'a diary contains information. Names and places and times.' She served out sausages and potatoes with practised ease.

Ben considered this in silence until he'd eaten the whole of his first sausage. 'Bel,' he said eventually, 'I take it all back. That's exactly it.'

'What?'

'Names and places and times.'

'Explain,' Jane ordered.

'Explosion,' Ben said, between mouthfuls. 'Blowing somebody up. IRA terrorists. Who's important? Who's coming who isn't normally here? Answer, the Bishop. Tomorrow night's carol service. It was all on the notice-board outside the church, except that it didn't make sense then.'

'It doesn't now,' Isobel said.

'Oh, yes, it does. You didn't hear what they said up on Cole's Hill. I did. You didn't hear what they said in the church this morning. Jane and I did. So there.'

'But you can't blow up a Bishop!'

'I'm not trying to,' Ben said reasonably. 'They are.'

'You can't *know.*'

'What other explanation is there?'

Isobel got up to fetch the apple pie and custard. 'We'll have to tell someone,' she said at length.

'Who? Beryl? She's frightened of two inches of snow. Good thing, really,' Ben said thoughtfully. 'Otherwise, we'd have had her round our necks all weekend. As it is, we have you, Bel.' He grinned. Flattery was painless, and sometimes effective.

'The police.'

'They wouldn't believe a word of it,' Jane said.

Ben considered this. Jane, for all that she spent most of her time with her head in a book, had a lot of common sense. He didn't particularly want to find himself being laughed at by a bunch of blue-uniformed flatties who would probably think their legs were being pulled and resent it. No, he had to have evidence to go on first, something hard and solid, not just guesses. And that meant going back to Cole's Hill. He glanced speculatively at Isobel. It was going to need careful handling, this little problem.

Meanwhile, there was the washing-up to do. Every little helped. He'd better be careful not to break any more cups.

As he ran the water into the sink, he looked at the garden. Footprints. That was where it had all started. Footprints in the snow. Those from yesterday were almost invisible now, covered with another dusting of shiny whiteness. But there was another set, big, clean, and recent, coming straight over the garden up to the back door.

Ben's shoulders stiffened. He grabbed the frying-pan, which was the only weapon handy, and marched to the door.

He was more annoyed than frightened. If they were going to start attacking in broad daylight, they had another think coming . . .

He threw open the door and stood there with the frying-pan raised for a quick knock-out blow.

'The blessing of Heaven and St Michael be on you,' said a rich Irish voice. Bright eyes twinkled under a woollen cap.

'Oh, it's you,' Ben said.

'And who were you expecting? The Devil, or just the gasman?' St Michael's worn lined face split into an ingratiating smile, and Ben's did the same. St Michael was an idle old beggar, but there was no harm in him.

'There's a cup of tea going, if you like,' Ben offered.

'Just what I was hoping for. Nothing stronger, I expect?

No, that would be asking too much of the Almighty's goodness. Will the lady of the house let me in for a while?'

Isobel graciously nodded her permission, and St Michael ostentatiously scraped the last vestige of snow off his scarred boots before he came in. He sat by the fire with a mug clasped in his hands and gently steamed. He gossiped about birds and animals, things that he knew about, and the strange ways of what he called this wicked world, with all the joy of a born countryman. He had no use for modern inventions.

He had been there for ten minutes, and had thanked Isobel for his mug of tea as though she were the squire's lady, when he rose to go.

'St Michael never outstays his welcome. He doesn't like four strong walls, either. If the good Lord had meant a man to live in a house, he'd have given him a shell like a snail.'

Ben laughed. 'And the thrushes would have grown a hundred times as big.'

'Ah, nature always has the last word. You can tramp across a ploughed field, and the rain will come and soften the marks till not even a robin could see them. The snow is a great coverer of man's mistakes. I noticed your telephone wire was down. A little snow, you see, and all the glory of man is but dust.'

'It won't take them long to mend it,' Isobel said.

'Don't you be so sure of that. Wire on a pole is a thing against nature. There are those who lay it on the ground. That's more respectful to the old folk who used to live on Cole's Hill.'

Ben's interest was suddenly caught. 'Cole's Hill? Wire?'

'Did I not say so? They didn't want to be seen doing it, but there's not much that escapes me. The blessing of Heaven be on this house.'

'Hoy!' Ben exclaimed. 'You can't go yet. What wire? And where?'

'I doubt if the shepherd ever had a telephone to go ring-ading-ding on Cole's Hill.'

'The shepherd's hut?'

'Look for yourself, if you wish.' With another of his lop-sided grins, St Michael slipped through the door and was gone, leaving behind him only his footprints in the snow.

'Well, well!' said Jane.

'I'm going out,' Ben announced.

Isobel looked at him suspiciously. 'Not by yourself.'

Ben groaned. 'It's cold,' he said. 'Freezing. Nasty wind. Chilblains. Red noses.'

'Wellingtons and a good big coat.'

'You'll get wet.'

'No more than you.'

Morosely Ben waited while Isobel and Jane dressed themselves up with so many clothes they began to look like suet dumplings with a pickled onion on top for a head. He told them so, but it made no difference. Ben wrapped his old scarf four times round his neck and was ready.

'Boots,' Isobel said sternly.

'OK, OK. Boots, boots, boots, boots, marching up and down again. You two will be the death of me.'

'We don't have that sort of luck.'

Ben let them have the last word.

It was certainly cold, out on the slopes of Cole's Hill. About a mile away, nearer the village, they could see little coloured dots skimming down and toiling back up again, bringing their sledges behind them. Ben wished he could join them, but now that Isobel had come, he felt obliged to keep his mind on the job.

'If St Michael saw this wire he was talking about, then it must be visible,' he muttered. They had spent an hour already in a biting wind, and had found nothing more exciting than an empty beer bottle.

'It'll be covered by the snow,' Jane said.

'Depends when they laid it. Strikes me they've been here only a day or two. They might have done it just before the snow came, but St Michael never mentioned it before, and it doesn't fit in with what I heard up by the hut. So there ought to be some pretty obvious disturbance on the ground, if only we could see it.'

'As it is, it's just us and the birds and the rabbits.'

'Another half-hour, and then we'll give it up.'

'We'll find it,' Isobel said firmly. 'We'll look until we do.'

Ben was surprised, but he said nothing.

They came upon it quite by chance, in a deep dell hidden by trees, where the snow was no more than a light scattering. A few bits of blackened wood showed where a fire had been lit at the bottom of the dell. Ben kicked around at the snow, and his foot caught in something which at first he thought was a bramble.

'Got it!' he yelled. 'I told you I was right.'

'Oh, yes?' Jane said. 'And who told *you*?'

'Wire. Coming down the hill towards the village. It's a long way, though. Must be miles of it. Getting on for half a mile to the hut on top, and more that a mile to the first house.'

'It's not just telephone wire, is it?' Jane sounded doubtful. 'Ours was brought down by the snow, remember.'

They looked at the wire as it lay, almost invisible on the ground. It was a light grey in colour, thin, innocent.

Isobel called out from the place where the fire had been. She was holding a soggy scrap of paper in her hand.

'I found it just by the side here. They must have used most of it to start the fire with, but this page escaped.'

They crowded round.

'It's a page out of a diary all right,' Ben said. 'You can't read the words, though.'

'There's one thing,' Jane pointed out. 'It's green ink.'

## *Chapter Eight*

It took them almost an hour to get back to the house, partly because of the snow which had again begun to fall, and partly because Ben insisted on finding out whether the ice on the stream was thick enough for skating. It wasn't. He also discovered that the stream was deeper than his wellingtons, and that did not improve Isobel's temper.

When Ben saw the house, black and low against the vast expanse of snow, he almost expected to find it broken into, even occupied. It had occurred to him, at about the same time that he found out his socks were not waterproof, that what the three on Cole's Hill were doing was not a joke. He wished the phone was working, but as it wasn't, they would have to fend for themselves. Once he had decided that, everything else seemed to fall into place.

He opened the back door cautiously, but there was no sign of life. Isobel pushed past him and switched on the light.

'Just in time,' she said. 'In another ten minutes it'll be dark outside.' She began to fuss around the kitchen with mugs and a kettle and a bottle of milk from the fridge.

Ben went on a tour of the house, armed with a stick which he picked up from the hall. It was as well to be prepared, but he needn't have bothered. Everything was just as they had left it, so far as he could see, but the feeling of something being wrong still lingered in the back of his head. It was almost as though he was being watched. He glanced over his shoulder, but it was only Jane looking at him with amusement.

'Gee!' she said. 'You looking for trouble, Batman?'

Ben ignored her.

Isobel was in a better mood when he came down, mainly because he had done nothing about his wet socks and she had the pleasure of telling him to go back up and change them. She chattered quite happily with Jane about what was on the telly and what they'd have for supper. Ben let them get on with it. He wandered from window to window, peering into the twilight. There were no footprints apart from their own, and even these were gradually being covered by the gentle snow. It all looked very pretty, Ben thought, but there was a threat in it somewhere. That feeling in the back of his head would not go away.

'The trouble is,' he said suddenly, 'nobody would ever believe they'd do it, and I'm beginning to wonder myself.'

Jane was bored with cooking and was ready to change the subject. 'Cole's Hill?'

Ben sat at the table with a mug of steaming tea and made patterns with biscuit crumbs. 'You can't just go and blow up a church.'

'Why not?'

'People don't. Not even terrorists.'

'One of them had an American accent, remember.'

Ben shrugged irritably. 'All right. So there's a wire going down from the hut to the village. The detonator will be in the hut, so they can just sit there in comfort while the balloon goes up.'

'The balloon being the church.'

'It sounds less and less likely every time I think about it.'

'Maybe it's not the church they're after.'

'They were there this morning.'

'They could have been checking on times and arrangements, that sort of thing.'

Ben considered this. The thing he really had to know was where the wire ended, and that involved another expedition. Once he knew that, he could simply cut the wire, or would that set off the explosion? There was so much that he did not *know* – but he meant to find out.

He glanced at Isobel.

'No,' she said firmly. 'You're staying in this evening.'

Ben decided to put up a fight. The battle raged for nearly a quarter of an hour, with Jane being umpire, and at the end of it Ben was pleased. He had succeeded in convincing Isobel that he had meant to use the evening for his investigation, and she would be on the alert to stop him. Once she thought she'd won, Ben would be free to act. He had no intention of wandering about in the pitch darkness – he needed light. He was going to wait until the first light of morning, and nobody would see him go.

He didn't have to pretend to be tired. He needed sleep, and he went upstairs early.

The alarm clock he had put under his pillow woke him an hour before dawn. He slipped out of the house like a grey ghost, making no sound. He had used the front door, because nobody else ever did, and with luck they wouldn't see the marks he made in the snow. Small hard flakes were still fluttering in the still air, and the sky was dark with just a faint glow in the south east, just enough to see by.

Ben trudged along the lane to the path which led to Cole's Hill. He would have to start from the dell where they had first found the wire, and work from there. He began to run.

Within twenty minutes he was there. Dawn had not yet come to the rough clearing among the trees, and Ben stood for a moment trying to pierce the blackness. Nothing moved. His eyes circled the clearing. Just as it had been last night – disturbed snow lightly covered and bushes weighed down into unnatural lumps.

He began to work his way up the hill, following the wire which he could trace by the disturbance in the snow. He tried to keep his own footprints within the bounds of that disturbance, but he was not always successful. The light was beginning to improve now, and he could see what he was doing.

When he came out of the belt of trees, the earth ramparts

reared above him like some great prehistoric monster asleep. He climbed the steep bank, ran into the ditch, and tried to use the momentum he gained to push him up the second bank. He stopped before he reached the top, so that his eyes could just see over the sparkling rim of the snow-covered rampart. At once he ducked down.

The shepherd's hut was no more than a hundred yards from him. The door was open, and a man was standing in front of it. The smoke of his cigarette hung in a cloud round his head.

Again Ben raised his eyes. The man was looking away now, and Ben was sure he had not been seen. He watched the little window by the side of the door, but nothing stirred.

So far then, Ben reflected, he was right. The wire went from the hut down to the dell among the trees. He now had to trace it in the other direction.

He ran through the drifts in the ditch between the two ramparts, kicking up great clouds of powdery whiteness which gleamed in the morning sun. The sky was clearing now, and the snow had ceased to fall.

He didn't stop at the dell, but carried on down to the valley, keeping an eye all the time for the line of disturbance which revealed the wire. Once or twice he uncovered it, just to make sure, then kicked the snow back into place. He reached the road almost before he realized where he was.

Ben stopped, looked up and down, noted the wheel-marks of the few cars which had passed. The wire presumably ran along the ditch by the side of the hedge. He ploughed into the snowdrift to find it, and couldn't. Annoyed, he hoisted himself up, shook the loose snow off his clothes, tried again further along. No luck.

In desperation he raced back into the wood to find the line and follow it more carefully. It could hardly just vanish, he told himself, but the trouble was that the snow concealed everything, and he didn't have time to go all the way back to the dell. He wanted to be home before Bel noticed his absence.

He found the drain by accident. Suddenly the snow gave way beneath him. His hands scrabbled for a hold and his feet kicked, and abruptly he was looking at a low arch made of brick, leading under the road. He peered in, but all he could see was a puddle of dirty water and then some sort of square crate. The wire showed as a thin grey line across the dirty snow.

Ben sat back on his heels. There it was, he said to himself, a box of explosive. A bomb. It would be detonated from the hut on Cole's Hill. He tried to imagine what the road would look like when the bomb went off. A crater, the wreckage of a car, people dead. Jane had been right. The church was not the place for the explosion, but the road here, just where the Bishop's car would pass on its way to the church. The man he had heard in the church had been right, too. The Bishop would not be hearing the carols.

Meanwhile, what was he to do? Ten hours before the explosion. He couldn't cut the wire: even if he had brought a pair of pliers with him, there was more than a chance that the bomb would go off as soon as the metal bit into the wire, and he didn't want to be around when that happened. He could tell the vicar, or the police, and be laughed at for his trouble. They probably wouldn't even believe him enough to come out and have a look. So anything that had to be done – Ben had to do it. So he told himself.

He was just about to turn and crawl out of the ditch when he heard the soft fall of feet in deep snow immediately behind him. He whirled round with his fists up, but a large hand gripped his neck and squeezed. His arms were caught and pulled behind his back, and he was dragged to his feet, his heels kicking empty air. He jerked his head back, felt it make contact with something yielding, heard a grunt of pain, was conscious of his arms being twisted until he thought they would drop off.

'Stand still, you little—'

A knee thumped into the small of his back, and he was sent sprawling in the snow. He squirmed to get up, but the breath had been knocked from his lungs, and he lay still.

Sounds came to his ears as though from an enormous distance. Boots shuffling through snow, the quick breathing of a man who had been running.

'Easy, Jed. No need to kill him.'

That was nice of them, Ben thought. He had to get up, but his muscles refused to work.

'Why not? Interfering kids.'

'It's the same one, Jed.'

'Think he knows anything?'

Ben kept his eyes closed and his hands still. If they thought he was unconscious, he might hear a bit more about their plans.

'He can't. Just a kid fooling about.'

'But what if he's seen something? He's been up by the wire. Footprints all over the place.'

Ben silently cursed the snow. It must have been easy for them to follow his prints, just as easy as for him to follow theirs.

'It won't matter after this evening.' The man laughed deep in his chest. 'We'll be away by six. With his nibs.'

'What do we do with him?'

A boot banged into Ben's ribs, but he kept his mouth closed and his body still. Hands came down, picked him up by the waist, slung him over a shoulder. Ben allowed himself to be carried. The man climbed out of the ditch, bumped him over a patch of rough ground. Through the slits of his eyelashes, Ben saw the ground rise and fall and tumble. Then he was thrown on to something soft. His head hit a solid metal bar and he fought to keep his senses in a well of starred black. Metal clanged.

'That'll keep him quiet' a voice said. 'Long enough.'

## *Chapter Nine*

At first he had no idea where he was. There was a smell of old leather in his nose, something like stale milk or an old English sheepdog, and there was pain in his arm. He tried to move his hands so that he could rub his wrists, but the pain became worse and he stopped.

When he opened his eyes he could see nothing but a mass of dirty brown material, curved like the back of an armchair. He puzzled over this for a moment while his senses gradually gathered information. There was light coming from somewhere, a gentle light which didn't hurt his eyes, but there was no sky above him, only a dim gloom as though he was in the middle of a forest. But there were no leaves, no sounds of branches - and no snow.

He was lying on his back, and his hands were underneath him, tied together with something that felt like his own scarf. He tried to sit up, but succeeded only in rolling over so that his head hit something solid, and his eyes closed again in a vain attempt to stop the thumping inside his skull.

For a minute he lay without moving. He was in a sort of square box with a metal framework which hurt when he hit it. Two small squares of light, like two eyes, were set in one of the sides. He remembered the drain under the road, and the box he had seen inside it, but that was far too small to be his prison now.

Somebody would come soon to let him out. They had to. They couldn't let him stay and rot inside this metal case for ever. Could they?

'That'll keep him quiet,' they had said. He remembered now. They had caught him while he was inspecting the wire which entered the drain, and they'd twisted his arms back and chucked him in here. 'Long enough,' they'd said. How long would that be?

Suddenly the realization came to him that nobody else knew where he was. Well, that was his own fault, and there was no use crying about it. Perhaps he should have left a note. Too late now.

The floor below him was solid, cold, smooth. He wriggled his way over it towards those two dim eyes, and bit by bit crawled into a sitting position with his back to them. That was better. He wasn't dead yet. Something like a round metal bar met the back of his hands, and he tried to work out what it was. He could feel it going all the way from the floor up his spine to the back of his head. It moved slightly as he struggled with the scarf around his wrists.

He had to do something about that scarf. He had never realized before how important the freedom of his hands was. Without the use of them, he felt the way a chicken must feel, all trussed up and ready for the oven. Except that the chicken was dead.

Ben laughed. That was better. It had not occurred to him before that he could use his lungs. He let out a great shout of 'Help!', but the noise seemed to re-echo round him, and he knew that it was unlikely to penetrate the walls of his prison. Still, somebody might hear. In all this snow? Early on a Sunday morning? If it *was* still Sunday morning.

Suddenly he felt hungry. He wondered whether the emptiness inside him meant that it was late in the day. Perhaps the explosion had already happened. Perhaps the three of them on Cole's Hill had already packed up and gone, their task finished.

Ben grinned to himself. He *always* felt hungry, so that didn't count as evidence. And it was still light. Those two eyes above him still glowed. He twisted his head round to look at them, and realization of what his prison was struck him like a pailful of cold water.

He was in a van, one of those mini-vans that you couldn't stand up in, with two doors at the back and a window at the top of each. He felt better now that he knew that much. His head was clearing, too, and the thumping inside sounded more like a distant door-knocker than a dirty great hammer. If he could get his hands free, he stood a chance of forcing the bar which held the doors locked.

He worked away at the scarf round his wrists, but it was tight and he couldn't get his fingers to the knots. It seemed like hours before he gave it up, realising that all he was doing was to increase the pressure on his wrists and make the knot tighter. Ben sat and thought for a moment to get his breath back.

Perhaps he could rub it up and down on that metal bar at his back? He tried it, but the bar was smooth and made no impression. Something sharp was what was needed. It was his best scarf, knitted by Isobel for him last Christmas, but it would have to go. She could always knit him another . . .

He edged over to the side of the van where the struts presented a sharper edge, and got himself balanced on his toes and knees so that he could scrape the scarf against the metal. For a second or two he thought he'd done it, but the scarf was tougher than he expected and his bonds seemed no less tight. He renewed his efforts, thinking that he had no time to waste, and scraped his arm rather than the scarf, but a few drops of blood were not going to stop him now.

At length he knew that it wasn't working. He could scrape away all day – all night? – and still he'd be tied as tight as ever. His fingers were going numb, and his arms as well, and he had to fight against the panic rising in his chest. His body was one whole mass of aching pains.

One sharp pain in particular was skewering him from behind. At first he thought he must be sitting on something sharp, the end of a bolt perhaps, or a stone. But then he realised, and he cursed himself for a fool.

He had a pen-knife in the back pocket of his jeans. That was what was sticking into him. A knife. Hope began to flood back into his head.

It took him several minutes to inch the knife out of his pocket, to hold it in his numb fingers, to ease the blade open. It was worth a broken fingernail to feel the edge of that blade. He turned the knife upwards, started sawing at the scarf like a tree-feller gone mad. The knife slipped from his grasp, and he cursed and started all over again. More slowly this time, with more care than fury. All his senses were concentrated on what his fingers were doing behind his back.

Gradually the woollen strands began to part. He could pull his arms wider now, feel the slackening of the knots, and there was a grin on his face. When he had done it, he sat for a minute and looked at the remains of the scarf, while he rubbed life back into his wrists and eased the pins and needles out. Isobel was not going to be pleased, he knew that. Perhaps he could spin some yarn about being attacked by wild foxes, mad with hunger in the frozen wastes of Cole's Hill, and fighting them off with his trusty pocket-knife. Perhaps not.

He was still hungry, even more hungry now. His mind was full of a vision of crisp bacon and fried eggs with a frill of brown lace round them, and great hunks of fried bread dripping with fat. He was looking forward to that.

First, though, he had to get out of this confounded van. He stood up with abrupt determination, and his head hit the roof and an explosion of stars inside it made him remember the need for caution. Those three thugs might still be around somewhere, and he didn't want to have to go through all this business again.

Quietly he applied himself to the double doors at the back, but they were firm. The round metal bar which ran from top to bottom was solidly based and moved no more than a fraction of an inch. There would be a lock on the outside, Ben thought, and those three had made certain that the key was turned.

'That'll keep him quiet,' they had said, and they'd meant it.

He was about to put his shoulder to it when something made him stop. His muscles tensed and his hair stiffened.

A tiny scrabble of noise outside.

Ben looked round for a weapon, but the floor was bare except for an old rug, and he had nothing but his hands and the blade of a pocket-knife. He was expecting any moment that the doors would burst out, and he'd be revealed while they stood there and laughed at him. He pressed himself against the sides of the van, ready to spring. The knife was clutched in his hand, and the blade glittered in the dim light.

Then he felt foolish. So a bird had walked over the top of the van, had it? Or a lump of snow had fallen off a branch. Gradually he became aware of the bumping of his heart and the tightness of his grip on the knife. And nothing had happened, after all. Still, he ought to be careful about the noise he made, even though there was no reason why the three thugs should hang around in the neighbourhood. Obviously they thought they had dealt with him and could now get on with whatever plan they intended to put into action.

Well, Ben said to himself, they were going to have to think again.

He moved the round metal bar experimentally. It squeaked a little, and for a second his fear returned. He strained his ears to pick up any sound from outside. A little gust of wind, a dead leaf bowling along the frosted earth – nothing more.

Ben still had the knife in his hand. He tried to ease out the rubber seal round one of the windows, but he soon realized that he would need a brick to remove the glass, and even if he had one, it meant noise. He had his boots, of course, but

to use them on the glass, even if they did the job, would set alarm bells ringing for miles around. If only it thundered, he thought. A good storm would cover the sounds he made breaking out, and he had never minded getting wet.

If he wrapped the torn remains of his scarf round his fist, perhaps he could break it that way. He would have to chance the noise being heard. With care he covered his knuckles with layers of wool and let fly at the glass. The jar ran up his arm like an electric shock, and his shoulder jerked and thudded as though he had broken a bone, but the glass remained whole.

Ben cleaned the dirt off the window and gazed out at the white world. Trees, bushes bowed down by the snow, a few more flakes fluttering down to fill up the holes on the ground. Footprints, disturbed and indistinct.

He tried to see round the corners, to get as wide a view as he could, but nothing met his gaze exept the sort of wintry scene, unpeopled, which one would expect to see only on a Christmas card.

A robin hopped across the icy surface and was gone.

Suddenly Ben was furious. Here he was, stuck in a van, when outside there were things to do, things which might mean life or death to someone who had never done anyone any harm, so far as he knew. More important, the van in which he was imprisoned might be blown sky-high as well.

With a sort of daft desperation he backed to the other end of the van, then launched himself at the doors. He was going to get through them, or knock himself out in the attempt.

As he neared the doors, he instinctively turned his head away, and it was his shoulder, already smarting, which took the force of the blow. He expected to go down, to sink into black unconsciousness, but instead he found himself flying on, out into the chilly air. The metal bar, held only at one end, had buckled just enough to allow the doors to swing wide.

Ben went sprawling in the snow, all the breath knocked out of his body. He lay and gasped and spluttered, with his face in a drift, and his hands clawing at the ground.

He lifted his head an inch or two, opened his eyes, stared.

A pair of boots, old, large, sprinkled with snowflakes, stared back at him.

# Chapter Ten

*'St Michael and all his angels defend us!'*

The words which filtered into Ben's brain made no immediate sense, but they were wonderfully familiar. Ben scrambled to his knees, hugging his shoulder, then to his feet, and saw St Michael himself, looking like a discarded scarecrow. Bits of newspaper appeared at the collar and cuffs of his ragged old greatcoat which was tied round his waist with a length of orange rope. He had made a hat for himself out of a cereal packet, and a scarf of a dirty brown colour was wrapped round his neck like a snake.

'My, but it's cold,' he said conversationally.

Ben handed him the remains of his scarf. 'Any use?'

The old man took the frayed knitting, gave it an admiring inspection, and added it to the one he already wore, so that his head looked as though it was sprouting through a heap of tyres. 'The blessing of Heaven,' he said. 'And where have you sprung from?'

Ben was wary. Old St Michael was Irish, and so were two of the thugs who had occupied Cole's Hill, and the connection between them might be closer than appeared. St Michael spent his days walking and observing: there wasn't much he didn't get to know.

'Out of that van,' Ben said. He was still rubbing his aching shoulder.

'And I thought I heard strange noises, like a cat caught in a coal-house. That's odd, I said to myself, and I kept watch. Rum things go on, don't they?'

'Oh, yes?'

The old man's eyes twinkled, and brown teeth showed in

his straggling beard. 'But you wouldn't be knowing about the gunpowder on the hill, would you?'

Ben looked up quickly. 'So you *do* know about those men.'

'St Michael has his ways and means. Two sons of Patrick and one of the colonies across the water.'

'You've seen them?'

'Oh, aye.'

'Spoken to them?'

'The time of day. A man has to be civil to his neighbours.'

Ben thought. He was still not sure about St Michael. 'What about the Bishop?'

'The Bishop of Rome, is it? Now there's a great and good man, for all he's not Irish.'

'Not him. The one who's coming this evening.'

St Michael shook his head, and a shower of dry snow fell from his cardboard hat.

'Thanks, anyway. I've got to get home. Do you know the time?'

'God's, or the BBC's?'

'Either.'

'An hour after sunrise. A beautiful time of day, though I could wish for a little more warmth from the old sun.'

Ben's heart lifted. It was still early in the morning, and he had plenty of time to get organised. If he hurried, he might even be back home before Bel noticed his absence.

'Cheerio,' he called out.

'The blessing of Heaven,' the old man said, raising a hand.

Ben ran all the way. By the time he got there, he was warm, pink, and puffing. Isobel was busy at the grill on the top of the oven, and there was a smell in the kitchen which made Ben forget everything else. He slipped into his place as though he had just come downstairs. He pretended a yawn to add a bit of colour to his acting, but Isobel was not deccived.

'You've still got your boots on,' she told him. 'And they're covered with snow.'

'He's just come in from Russia,' Jane said. She had a book on the table as usual, but she had taken in Ben's appearance with one quick glance. 'Walking all the way.'

'Shut up,' Ben said, but he got up, removed his boots, and found a pair of dry sandals.

'Well?' Isobel demanded.

Ben considered. He *could* keep quiet about this morning's little adventure, say nothing at all, play dead. But that would mean that Bel would nag him for the rest of the day, and he was going to need her help. He decided to come clean.

'I went out early to trace that wire,' he began.

'I saw you,' Jane put in. 'But it looked cold, so I went back to bed.'

So much, Ben thought, for his ability to slip in and out of the house without being noticed. He might just as well have slammed the door.

'You slammed the door,' Jane said.

Ben glared. 'Are you telling this story, or am I?'

'Carry on, big brother.'

Isobel brought over a plate of bacon and eggs and the remains of the fried potatoes. 'And make it the truth,' she said. 'The tea's in the pot.'

Ben took a mouthful, swallowed, took another. 'The wire goes to the hut, that's for sure. I traced it up to the ramparts. Those men are back in the hut, by the way. I saw one of them.'

'Did they see you?'

'Well, I suppose they must have. Or my footprints in the snow. You can't do a thing out there without leaving marks. Nuisance. Well, then I followed it down the hill to the road, and there it stopped. At least, I think it did.'

'Either it did or it didn't. Which?'

'It went into the ditch and then into a drain which goes under the road. I couldn't see much, except for a square sort of box in this big round pipe.'

'Explosive?' Jane asked.

'I didn't have time to find out. I was going to look if the wire came out on the other side, but I got nabbed.'

'But with one bound, Batman, you were free.'

'Shut up, Jane, and listen!'

'Only trying to cut the story short.'

Ben pushed his empty plate away. 'I needed that. Well, there was one of the thugs right behind me, and they bundled me into this van. When I woke up, I was locked in, and tied up with that scarf of yours, Bel.'

'The idea!' Isobel said with annoyance. 'All the time I spent knitting that. Where is it now?'

'Safe enough,' Ben said evasively. 'The important thing is that I managed to get out—'

'With one bound? Gee, Batman—'

'Will you shut up!' Ben roared. 'It took a lot of energy and hard work, I'll tell you. My arms still hurt, and so does my shoulder.' If he was playing for sympathy, he got none. Jane looked hurt and pointedly turned a page of her book.

'Are you telling me,' Isobel demanded, 'that those men on Cole's Hill shut you up in a smelly dirty *van?*'

'Well, yes, but I got out—'

'That's not the point. You might have been killed.'

Jane produced a short noise of derision, but seeing the look on Isobel's face said nothing more. Isobel was clearly furious. As the oldest of the three, she considered herself responsible for the welfare of them all.

'We shall have to tell the police,' she insisted.

'The line's down,' Ben reminded her. 'It won't have been repaired yet. And what's the point? It'd take us all our time to get over to the police station and they wouldn't believe us even if we told them.'

'Beryl?' Jane suggested.

Ben snorted. 'You know what she's like. She'd dither like a wet hen.'

'So what do we do?'

'I had a bit of an idea,' Ben said modestly.

'Well?'

Ben spent the next ten minutes explaining. At first he was greeted with howls of mockery, but he ploughed on until eventually even Isobel was beginning to agree with him. It involved a lot of foot-work, but as Jane said, they had the whole day.

'Right,' Ben said. 'I'll get started.'

'I could do with the fresh air,' Jane suggested.

Ben looked at her with horror.

'Well, why not?' she said. The alternative, after all, was to stay at home and be ordered about by Isobel who had big plans for the midday meal.

'Back by one,' she said before Isobel could think of anything to stop her.

Outside, the sky was blue and the air cold. The snow was topped with a thin layer of ice which crunched enjoyably under their feet. They skirted Cole's Hill, keeping to the tracks made by cars along the road. They passed no one, and no car disturbed the quiet of the morning, broken only by church bells in the distance.

'Do you think he'll help?' Jane asked as they came to the village and walked along the street.

'If I know Drako, he will.' Ben sounded confident.

'There'll be a lot of trouble.'

'Always is. Drako won't mind that. He runs that place. Sort of shop steward.'

'H'm.'

'Don't h'm, just follow,' Ben said severely. He led the way through the lychgate into the churchyard where the tombstones stood up like iced fingers in a white ground, round to the back of the church where there were dustbins full of dead flowers and a tiny tough door with an enormous black iron ring.

'Won't be long,' Ben said comfortably, leaning on a dustbin.

They could hear the singing of the last hymn, the vicar's blessing, and the playing of the organ as the congregation chattered and formed in groups by the main porch. A few minutes later the little door by Ben's side burst open and a boy with bright red hair and a fierce expression came out with his hands in his pockets.

'Hi, Drako.'

'Oh, it's you.' Drako's face never smiled, not even when as senior choir-boy he was singing in church.

'We need help,' Ben began.

'Try the Brownies,' Drako said, with a quick look at Jane.

'Don't you be rude about my Brownies,' Jane objected.

'Come over here,' Ben said. This was no time for a fight between Drako and Jane. A crowd of boys and girls fanned out from the door, glad to use the snow as ammunition after being cooped up inside for the best part of an hour. Jane found herself involved: she was not one to take a snowball in the face lying down. Ben and Drako were lost to view. When the choir had gone its cheerful way, Jane still stood there, panting and cross.

'You look warm,' Ben said. 'It's all fixed. Drako will do it. When he gives the signal, everybody out. Anything for a bit of excitement, he says.'

'Oh? And who gives him the signal?'

'I've thought of that. We've got a couple of big rockets left over from Guy Fawkes. They'll do.'

'We were saving those for my birthday,' Jane said dangerously. She wasn't keen on choir-boys at the moment.

'I'll buy you another,' Ben offered.

Jane laughed with disbelief. 'You and who else?'

Drako came over and slapped her on the shoulder. 'Him and me, kiddo. Either you co-operate, or you stay at home and watch the telly.'

Jane was so furious that she could find nothing sufficiently biting to say. Ben grinned, and that was no help.

'Cheese it, the cops!' Drako suddenly exclaimed. His conversation consisted almost entirely of phrases picked up from the comics he read under the book-rest during the sermons.

Ben whirled round. Drako was right. 'Somebody's coming,' he muttered. 'Quick! Behind the dustbins.'

## *Chapter Eleven*

They crouched between the flint wall and the cold metal bins like three rats trapped in a corner. It was Drako who first broke the silence. 'Gee!' he said, expelling his breath in one great gasp. 'Had me worried for a minute, but it's only the boss. Hi, boss!' They stood up, tried to look innocent, and failed.

'Ah, William,' the vicar said. 'Who have we here? More recruits for the choir?'

Ben looked alarmed. 'Er – no,' he said. It was something he wanted clearly understood. 'Just visiting. Talking to Drako.'

'I am surprised you can get a word in edgeways,' the vicar remarked with a touch of bitterness. 'I can hardly hear myself speak during the course of the service. I suspect that the choir lays bets on the length of the sermon.'

Drako's eyes widened. 'I never realised you knew.'

'I didn't, but I do now. Well, good day to you. Don't be late for Evensong. We rely on you, William. Remember that the Bishop will be there. We need to put on a good show – er, that is, to raise a worthy song to the Lord.'

'What time is he coming?' Ben asked.

'The Bishop, or the Lord? Well, sometimes, I fancy it's the same person.'

'The time,' Ben prompted.

'Curiously enough, I know the answer to that. When my diary was stolen, I had no idea what was happening, so I had to telephone to make sure of the details. The Bishop is due at St Aldate's at 6.10 precisely.'

'So he'll be passing Cole's Hill at about six,' Ben said thoughtfully. 'It fits.'

'Does it? With what?'

'Evensong,' Drako said abruptly.'We'll be there, don't you worry.'

'I gave up worrying a long time ago so far as the choir is concerned,' the vicar said sadly. 'Only the Lord could cope with that.' He wandered away among the tombstones.

'Jammy so-and-so,' Drako muttered.

'All set, then?' Ben asked.

'Sure thing, kiddo. You can rely on the United States Marines.' Drako gave them a jaunty salute and ran off.

Ben and Jane followed more slowly. 'I'm hungry,' Ben remarked. 'It's all this fresh air and exercise. Come on, Jane.'

Their way took them past Cole's Hill. It looked clean and innocent in the bright sunlight of midday. The ramparts which encircled the top were like a great white wall.

Ben looked up and scanned the skyline, but there was nothing he could see that was odd or out of place. The shepherd's hut was well hidden.

They came to the place where the woods swept down the slope to the road. Ben wanted to break into a run, but he didn't like to seem scared when Jane was about, and he ambled along deliberately slowly.

'It was just about here,' he said airily. 'The wire comes through those trees, down into the ditch, and then into this sort of drain.'

'Where?'

'You're not looking, Jane. It's there, right under your feet.'

'All right, so I'm being blind.'

With a sigh Ben jumped down into the ditch to prove it to her. He spent a minute or two kicking snow about, and then he hauled himself out, a frown on his face.

'Funny. It *was* there. They were going to set off the bomb just here, about six o'clock, just when the Bishop was passing.'

'Well, if it isn't there now, that means we've frightened them off. They know the plan's no good, so they've gone. Vamoosed.'

Ben looked disappointed. 'They wouldn't give up that easy. Not them. Just think for a minute. They think I'm onto them, so they shut me up in that van, and then they're in the clear. Why should they just disappear?'

'Because they found out you'd escaped.'

Ben glanced uneasily over his shoulder, but there wasn't a soul in sight. Still, they had better be getting home, or Bel would be cross again. He began walking.

'Hang on' Jane said. 'Where *is* the van?'

Ben pointed vaguely in the direction of the woods.

'Let's have a look, then. We've got plenty of time.'

Reluctantly Ben followed her into the shadows of the trees. His eyes darted this way and that, alert to pick up any sign of movement.

The van was behind a line of bushes, well-covered and hidden, but no more than twenty yards from the road. Ben grabbed at Jane's arm.

'Somebody's been here,' he muttered. 'I know I left those back doors open, and they're shut now.'

'Old St Michael?' Jane suggested.

'Doubt it. Those three must have come back, so they *do* know I escaped.' Ben's eyes wandered ceaselessly round the ring of trees. Jane was more interested in the van. It was old and rusty and obviously abandoned, though it still had its tyres.

'Plenty of wire,' she remarked. 'It's all bundled up inside. You can see through the window.'

Ben was looking inside the windows at the front. 'This old heap of rust won't ever move again,' he said. 'Anything else in the back?'

'Not that I can see. It's all dark, and the glass is smeary. Ben, what did that crate you said was in the drain look like?'

Ben wandered round to the back and looked in. 'It might

be that thing in the corner. Let's have a go at the doors.' He pulled at the handle, but nothing gave. 'They've obviously locked it,' he said, 'and a bit better than last time, too.'

'Ben, I've had an idea.'

'Oh?'

'What about trying to divert them from the top of the hill? We can't start playing about with this wire, because we don't really know what it's for, and the whole thing might go up in one enormous bang, but if we could get them away from Cole's Hill, that would do as well, wouldn't it?'

'How?'

Jane frowned. 'You could throw a stone with a message tied round it, saying "All is discovered. The cops are on the way. Fly! Signed, Patrick O'Grady".'

'Any other bright ideas?'

'You could lead them off on a chase in the opposite direction and shut them up in a ruined castle.'

'They run faster than I do. They've proved it.'

'Even the short fat one?'

'It's the other two I'm worried about.'

'Are you scared, Ben?'

'Yes,' Ben said simply.

'Well, I think we ought to go up there and have a look, anyway.' With a toss of her hair, Jane was off and running before Ben could stop her.

'Hi!' he yelled, but she took no notice. Grimly he started in pursuit. She'd ruin everything, he was thinking, as he panted along behind. Jane could run as fast as he could, if she put her mind to it, and she had a good start.

He lost her through the trees, and he stopped to listen. He could hear the soft thud of feet in snow, but it seemed to be coming from behind him. Nervously he looked round, but there was nobody that he could see. An echo, perhaps. He moved on, trying to pick up her footprints, and eventually found them, but by this time, he thought, she must be almost at the top. Ben cursed and began again to run.

When he reached the top of the first rampart, he saw her high on the second one waving. He almost shouted, but stopped himself in time. Her back was towards him. Slowly and softly he went down the ditch and up the steep slope of the second rampart until his eyes could just see over the mounds of frozen snow. A short fat blob of a man was standing at the door of the shepherd's hut. The smoke from his cigarette hung over his head, but his hands were still.

Ben froze as he glanced over to Jane. She was thirty yards to his right, and as he watched, she began to amble carelessly down the bank on which she had been standing and make for the hut. She was more than half-way across the level surface before she stopped. Ben heard her shout but could distinguish no words.

Ben's mind was in turmoil. He could not imagine what she thought she was doing, walking straight into a trap like that, after all that he had told her about his early morning capture and lucky escape. His whole body was as tense as a spring.

The man had started moving now, slow short steps in Jane's direction. He threw the cigarette into the snow and his arms swung at his sides. Again Jane shouted. The man stopped, said something that Ben couldn't hear.

A movement behind the hut caught his eye. Jane couldn't see, but one of the bigger taller men was there. Ben could imagine the glitter of his eyes.

Then all was confusion. In a riot of shouts and flying snow, the man behind the hut rushed forward. Jane paused for a second, and then she was off like a deer, hair flying and heels kicking. The short fat man stood as though struck by lightning, but the bigger man was moving, and moving fast, shortening the distance between himself and Jane with every thudding step.

One thought sprang into Ben's mind. Where was the third member of the gang? Well away and out of reach, or lying in wait somewhere near and ready to pounce? But Ben

had no time to worry about what he could not see. If Jane was not to be caught, he had to produce some sort of diversion.

He scrambled up to the top of the rampart, cheered, yelled, jumped, ran. The big man swerved, looked over his shoulder, almost slid on the icy surface. Then, with a great roar he ran for Ben who raced along the top of the rampart to his left for fifty yards before dropping down into the ditch and doubling back. He could hear the thump of the man's boots and knew that he had nearly reached the top. Desperately he buried himself in a deep drift and lay still, fighting for his breath and control over his jerking legs and arms. The footsteps slowed, pounded on, slowed again. Ben almost stopped breathing as he listened, expecting to find the man's boot any minute only an inch from his face.

The man had stopped again. Tension lay heavy on the air and in the drift where Ben lay. Then the thudding began again, but more distant now, and below the level of the rampart. Confused by the tracks, the man was following the line of prints Ben and Jane had made on the way up.

Ben gulped air into his lungs, grinned. Just occasionally some of his ideas worked out the way he wanted. At once he was up and running, flinging snow from him like a terrier digging for a rat, keeping to the bottom of the ditch and following the line of the rampart as it circled Cole's Hill.

As he turned a sudden corner and raced on, he banged into something solid. Noise filled his ears, shouts and clamour. Then he was rolling, with whatever it was he had run into clasped in his arms, rolling over and over and down and down until his face was covered in snow and his cheeks burned with its icy touch.

## *Chapter Twelve*

Ben came to an abrupt and jarring stop against a tree. At once he was up and running, straight for the cover of the woods. Not until he reached the lane at the bottom of Cole's Hill did he stop to think, to take in breath, and to look around him.

'Oh, it's you,' he said.

'Who did you expect?' Jane asked calmly. 'The Queen of Sheba?'

'What the blazes did you think you were up to?'

'Giving them something to think about. It worked, too.'

'You might have been caught, and Isobel would have blamed me.'

'Oh, hang Isobel. I enjoyed it.'

'What did you say to that man up there?'

'"Fly. All is discovered!" It worked in a book I was reading the other day. I've often wondered whether you could do the same thing in real life.'

'What did he say?'

'I'm not going to repeat that,' Jane said with a grin. 'Very educational. He was quite cross.'

'The point is, have we given them the slip?'

'If they come down Cole's Hill the way we did, we'd certainly know. They'd be screaming for help with a broken leg each.'

'Shut up and listen, Jane.' Ben looked at the empty lane. No sign of anyone there or in the woods, and no sound but the faint rattle of cold branches in the breeze.

'They've given up,' Jane announced confidently. 'You said you were hungry. So am I. Let's go and see what Isobel's got cooking.'

Isobel was all good temper when they trooped in. She gave Ben the usual telling off for not shaking all the snow off his jeans, but he had expected that and he took no notice of it.

'Smells good,' he said.

'Corned beef hash.'

'With onions?'

'Of course.'

Ben fell upon it like a starving python. Fresh air certainly sharpened the appetite. Between mouthfuls he told Isobel of what he had arranged with Drako, and, in an edited version, what had happened on Cole's Hill. He was quite happy to do the washing-up afterwards while Jane made a pot of tea.

Ben's mind was full of plans and possibilities. His hands were busy in the soapy water, but his eyes were gazing out of the garden. Suddenly he froze.

'Bolt the back door,' he said quietly. Jane moved to the door without a word and did as she was told, then joined Ben at the kitchen window above the sink. Ben pointed a finger. Jane looked out over the silent hidden garden to the belt of trees which bordered the field beyond. Dark tall trunks, branches each with a white line of snow, shadows at their roots. And among the shadows a slow definite movement.

Ben sighed. It was a complication, but one which he had half expected. 'Abandon ship' he ordered softly. 'Grab some food, Bel. Don't just stand there gaping like a goldfish. There were some Mars bars in the cupboard. Put 'em in a bag and look slippy. We've got about a minute.'

'But you haven't finished those plates,' Isobel objected.

Ben looked at her in silent wonder, but Jane was already busy with a bag.

'Warm clothes,' she said casually. 'It's going to get cold.'

'But what do they *want?*' Isobel demanded.

'Us,' Ben said simply. 'They were bound to come, I suppose. Drawn by the smell of your cooking, Bel. Come on. Out by the front door.'

There was just a possibility, he reflected, that the front door was being watched, but he doubted it. Nobody ever used it in the ordinary way, and he thought he had seen three shadowy figures among the trees. They had come in force.

They slipped out through the front door, closed it quietly behind them, and made for the little plantation of fir trees at the end of the next field. Footprints were a problem, Ben realised, but he got Jane and Isobel to run off in different directions and then double back in order to make it as confusing as he could. When they reached the plantation, they merged into the shadows like three thin ghosts. No snow had penetrated the thick dark foliage, and feet made no mark on the hard ground.

'Tree-house?' Jane said softly.

'Where else?'

Ben knew where he was going. Last summer he had spent a lot of time building a platform high up in one of the firs

which looked out towards the house. It had walls of sticks and cardboard, and an old green groundsheet for a roof. A rope ladder dangled by the side of the trunk.

One after another they climbed up, squatted on the rough platform, peered through the snow-heavy branches. Ben hauled up the ladder.

'They'll never find us now,' he muttered. Without the ladder dangling down, the tree-house was invisible from below.

'There's one of them,' Jane whispered. 'Just coming round the corner of the house.'

'I hope they're not going to do any damage,' Isobel said.

'Can't help that.' Ben shrugged his resignation. He knew his limitations. If those three thugs intended to break in, there was nothing that he or Jane or Isobel could do about it. He narrowed his eyes against the glare from the snow. The short fat man was standing in the front garden looking up at the windows. Then he went to the door, tried the handle. Ben heard him shout something. The sound bounced off the walls like a mountain echo.

A ragged scarecrow figure ambled into Ben's line of sight. He stiffened. 'What's he doing there?' he mumbled.

'Who?'

'St Michael.'

'He's Irish,' Jane said with finality. 'So are they. Course he knows them.'

Ben's suspicions grew. St Michael always seemed to be turning up. Perhaps he was just being nosy, the way he usually was, liking to know everything that went on, but there might well be something more sinister in his appearance now. He could have seen them as they slipped out by the front door. He might even know about the tree-house. There wasn't much his bright old eyes didn't notice and store away for later use. Ben wished he could hear what they were saying down there.

'Watch it!' Jane told him. 'You'll fall out.'

'Shut up!'

Ben kept his eyes fixed on the strange pair at the front of the house, as though by concentrating all his senses he might somehow divine what was going on. St Michael was waving his arms about and pointing. To the plantation? It almost looked like it. Ben's face set in a frown. If St Michael was on the side of the thugs on Cole's Hill, it was going to muck things up more than a bit.

One of the taller men joined the group. They stood there, squat, fore-shortened, like animated garden gnomes, looking into all the windows. One of them was smoking his French cigarettes, and Ben thought he could almost smell the scent of it. His nose twitched. He rubbed his hands together. He was beginning to realise how cold it was.

Short fatty was waddling across the front garden now, pushing the gate open, looking down the unused lane.

'He's seen the footprints,' Ben muttered. 'He's coming. No, he's not, though. He's going the other way, down to the stream, looks like. There's St Michael pointing again. That's the way he must have come himself. That helps. There's plenty of footprints to confuse them.'

They watched in fascination from their hide in the fir tree, as though the figures in the distance were part of a play put on for their entertainment. Short fatty had disappeared now, down the road beyond their sight, and St Michael was clinging on to the other man's arm, probably, Ben thought, asking for the price of a drink. He might even have some luck, too. St Michael was a persuasive old so-and-so. The two of them were at the corner of the house when the third man joined them. He had a spade in his hand and was waving one arm in the direction of the windows.

'Oh, no!' Isobel exclaimed. 'They can't do that!'

'You going to try to stop them?' Ben said casually.

'But there'll be glass everywhere.'

Ben's eyes were still on the group of three at the window. St Michael looked as though he was trying to persuade them not to use the spade, but the tall man shook him off and St Michael went sprawling in the snow. As he started to pull himself up, short fatty appeared again. He was running with short little steps and his breath hung in the air like a horse's. He was waving his arms and pointing down the road.

'There's a car coming,' Jane remarked. 'You can just hear it.'

'Can't be the milkman. He never comes on a Sunday, and anyway it's far too late for him.'

The gentle hum increased in volume, accompanied by a strange slithery noise which, Ben realised, was probably tyres sliding on the snow. Ben craned out of the tree-house to get a better view.

It was a small black car, old-fashioned and in need of a clean, and it came to a sliding halt outside the house. The sound of the engine died away, and they heard the sharp click of a door. Ben glanced back to the house. No sign of the three thugs. Only St Michael scrambling about in the snow and looking like something the cat had decided not to bring in.

Jane started giggling. 'It's Beryl,' she said. 'She's braved the snow after all.'

'Beryl the peril,' Ben said. 'She's going to walk straight into it.'

They watched as the short solid figure dressed in mauve marched through the front garden and up to the door. Beryl turned and seemed to be speaking to St Michael, who hurriedly pulled himself together and scuttled off round the corner. Beryl knocked at the door, waited, knocked again, then began to peer into the windows, and finally walked round to the back out of sight.

'That ought to cause a bit of a riot,' Ben commented.

But nothing happened. No voices raised, no sound of blows on a bolted door, no flying figures black against the snow.

'At least she's saved the windows,' Isobel said.

'So far.'

'And it'll probably do some good. If those three see that she can't get any answer either, they'll know we're not there and won't try to break in.'

'That depends what they're after.'

'Us. That's what you said. To keep us quiet.' Isobel shivered suddenly, and it wasn't just the cold.

'You may be right' Ben said. He sounded surprised. 'There's Beryl coming round again, so they haven't nobbled her.'

'They can't be that desperate,' Jane said with another giggle.

Ben silenced her with a glance of contempt. 'The point is, what's she going to do? She's got a key to the front door, so she'll go in, won't she? Yes, there she goes. Wait a minute or two. That didn't take long. I bet she's thinking some hard thoughts about the washing-up we didn't finish. Too bad. She's off again. Not much of a driver, is she? Slither, slide, grinding gears, another slide. There she goes. Blast!'

'What's up?' Jane demanded.

'I've just remembered. The rockets. We shall need those for signalling to Drako. And they're still inside the house. Blast!'

## *Chapter Thirteen*

'Ben! You're not to go back in!' Isobel was firm.

Ben did not bother to argue. 'Stay here,' he told them. 'Or I'll set Beryl on you.'

'But she's gone—'

So had Ben. Like a disturbed squirrel he was down the ladder before either of them could stop him. He could only hope that they would do as they were told. By himself he had a chance, but with them hanging around him, none at all.

He stood at the edge of the plantation, still under cover, while he watched and listened. No sign of life from the house, and, just as important, none from behind him. With eyes and ears alert, he crept along the ditch until he had gained the shelter of the tall overgrown hedge which ran along the side of the house. From there, peering through the snow-lined branches, he could see most of the back garden and keep an eye on the back door. It was shut, just as it had been left, and there was no evidence of a break-in.

So far, so good. Probably they had been convinced by Beryl's appearance and almost immediate departure that there was no one inside the house, and so they'd gone off back to Cole's Hill, taking St Michael with them, if he was really involved with their plot. Certainly, Ben could not see him or his tattered hat anywhere in the garden, though his view of the trees at the bottom was incomplete.

Well, he would have to chance it. He began to push his way under the hedge by means of a gap he had often used in the past. He was trying to be silent, and that was no easy matter when every movement dislodged a shower of powdery snow.

He was almost through when he stopped in sudden alarm. 'Blast!' he said again, and meant it. He had realized that the back door was bolted on the inside, and that the front door had been pulled to and Isobel had the key. Then a slow grin spread over his face. There was a way, if you looked hard enough to find it. A tree grew by the side of the house, and one of its bigger branches stretched across the wall towards the window of his own room. The little window at the top of the frame had never fitted properly: Ben knew that, even if the three men from Cole's Hill didn't.

Ben took a quick glance round the garden and at the line of trees at the bottom as he cautiously pushed himself through the last of the hedge and stood up. He could have wished for a little less light if he was going to play the part of a cat-burglar, but he couldn't wait much longer. Already the sun had gone beyond the trees, but the snow lying smooth and glistening in the garden reflected what light there was. He would look like a beacon as he crossed to the house, but there was nothing he could do about that. If anybody was watching, then he'd have to run for it, but he didn't *feel* as though he was being watched . . .

With impulsive resolution he ran to the shed which leaned against the side wall. If anyone was about, they'd have seen him by now. He climbed on to the rim of the water-butt, stretched up to the ridge of the shed roof. From there it was an easy swing to the lower branches of the tree. Snow fluttered and fell as he shifted to the branch which would take him to the window.

The frame yielded to the pressure of his fingernails, and he pulled it open and eased an arm inside to reach the catch of the big window. A sharp click made him freeze for a second, but there was no answering sound from below, and he began to edge the window open. One foot on the windowsill, one arm round the frame - easy as a knife through warm butter. A little snow followed him in and dribbled wetly on the carpet, but he had no time for that.

The thought struck him that he might be walking straight into a trap. They'd be downstairs, or maybe on the landing outside the door, with grins all over their faces and something solid in their hands. Waiting for him. And he, like a fool, running slap into them.

Quietly he stepped over to the door, put a hand to the door-knob. He almost expected to feel it turn of its own accord in his fingers. He looked round for a weapon, but all he could find was an old broken cricket bat. Still, it was better than nothing. He felt safer with the handle firmly in his grasp.

The door came towards him as he pulled, making soft noises as it scraped across the carpet. Ben held his breath. One eye peered through the widening crack. The landing was dark and empty. Ben breathed again.

He found the two rockets where he remembered putting them, on top of the wardrobe. They were bigger than he thought, and for a moment he wondered how he was going to keep them dry. Then he remembered the black plastic bags which were kept in the kitchen and were used to hold rubbish. One of those would do the trick, except that getting it meant going down through the shadows of the staircase to the kitchen. His hand went to the lightswitch but stayed there without pressing it down. In the twilight outside, a light in the window would look like a forest fire. Still, if it had to be done, then he'd better get it over.

The matches were in the kitchen, too. He was glad he had remembered those. The rockets would have been a fat lot of use if he hadn't.

Step by step he crept down the stairs. There was one that always creaked, seven from the bottom. He made a long stride and by-passed it, but the handrail to which he clung groaned instead. Ben began to wonder why he was scared. The house was empty, he knew that. It *felt* empty. The only sound was his own breathing, and the only smell the remains of the meal they'd had in the middle of the day. The mere thought of it made Ben hungry again. Perhaps he could pick up a Mars bar on the way through, and then he remembered that Isobel had them all. That's life, he told himself, just one thing after another.

The kitchen was dim, the window a white blur. He automatically put out a hand to the switch, but brought it back with a jerk just in time. He knew where the matches were usually kept, on a shelf by the side of the oven. His fingers felt along the smooth wood, found the box. It rattled as he picked it up.

Now for the black plastic bag. Under the sink, he thought, unless Isobel had been having another of her spring-cleaning fits. There was only one left, and he stuffed it under his arm. His need was greater than the dustman's.

Up the stairs again, counting the steps, waiting for the creak from the handrail, across the landing into the safety of his own room. With relief he shut the door and leaned against it.

It took him only a moment to wrap the rockets in the shiny plastic. The matches were safely in his back pocket. He turned to the window.

He was just about to put a leg over the sill and swing himself out to the branch when his eye caught something odd in the garden.

A scarecrow, where no scarecrow should be.

Down by the line of trees, deep in the shadows, a round figure with a long dirty coat and a straggling beard. The face was turned towards the house, and Ben thought that he caught the gleam of an eye beneath that squashed hat.

St Michael.

Ben drew back. The curtain flapped idly in the cool air which came through the open window. He tried to keep it still so that thc movement did not attract attention, but as he grasped it he knew he was too late. The curtain must have been flapping like that for the last ten minutes, and any fool could see the window hanging wide, even in this poor light.

The moon was beginning to rise over the trees, but the clear cold radiance served only to make the shadows at the roots of the trees even deeper.

Could he be sure it was St Michael, standing there like a weather-worn statue? And if it was, what in the name of all his fellow-angels did he think he was doing? Spying for those thugs on Cole's Hill, that was for sure.

Ben suddenly felt lonely. Not afraid, but separate, isolated. He had always had a soft spot for the old rogue with his over-done Irish accent and idle begging; he'd thought of him as a friend. Well, friends sometimes turned out to be enemies.

Ben brushed his mind clean of sadness. He had a job to do, and there was no time to waste. He could be thankful that it was only St Michael down there, left to keep guard by himself, rather than the whole gang. The three of them were probably in position right now, waiting for the count-down and blast-off. He had no time to worry about anything else.

One more quick glance into the garden told him that there were no other shadowy figures in that clump of trees. He swung out on to the branch, pushed the window shut, crawled along the main trunk, eased himself down on to the shed and the water-butt to the ground. He had to keep a tight hold on the rockets in their plastic bag, or he could have done the whole operation in half the time.

A quick spring to the hedge, down on hands and knees, through to the lane. Up and away. Feet slipping and sliding in the snow. Car tracks where the snow was compacted, like ice. Beryl's car. One set of tracks up to the house, an indistinct patter where she had backed and turned, another set returning.

But a third set as well.

Ben came to an abrupt stop. The lane went nowhere but to the old house in which they lived. After that, it ran on for about twenty yards, then dwindled away into ruts and puddles and a scrubby wood.

Another car had come this way, and had not gone back.

Ben's eyes swept the hedges, the front of the house, the bushes beyond. Cars don't just vanish, or take off and fly, leaving no wheel marks behind. Was that a square black shape up there among the trees? Or just a bush bowed down by the weight of snow?

Ben moved quietly, carefully, into the ditch. His legs sank into the drift, and he felt trapped. That was it – they'd been playing with him, just waiting out here, ready to grab him when he emerged. It had not been just St Michael on guard at the back. He'd been put there to drive him round to the front, into the expectant arms of the three from Cole's Hill.

He sensed the hair on the back of his neck prickle like a dog's. His grip on the rockets was so fierce he could feel the sticks bending, almost breaking. Panic rose in his chest like a great solid stone, forcing its way into his throat until he thought he'd have to let it out in one enormous yell.

'Come and get me!' he wanted to shout, but nothing came when he opened his mouth to scream.

If only he could see them, if only he knew the direction from which they would come to grab him, if only he had something in his hands to fight with, something stronger than rocket sticks which he could snap with two fingers—

Into his terror-struck head came a sound that turned his panic to laughter.

'Yoo-hoo, stranger!'

Nobody could yell in quite those tones. It had to be Jane. He had almost forgotten Jane and Isobel stuck up in the tree-house, waiting for him to come back until they grew tired of waiting and came to fetch him. Fear fell from him like a coat slipping from his shoulders. He *knew* there'd been someone there, waiting.

Jane and Isobel.

He could see them now, two small figures emerging from

the plantation, wrapped in scarves and thick pullovers and knitted hats. Their feet brushed through the snow in a steady comforting rhythm.

'You've been long enough,' Isobel said sternly.

'We got cold up there,' Jane went on, 'and nothing seemed to be happening, so we came on down. Got everything?'

'Sure,' Ben managed to croak. He wasn't going to tell them what he had been thinking. He had his pride.

'What are we waiting for, then? We ought to be there by now. Don't just stand around, Ben.'

Ben climbed out of the ditch, fighting against the snow, but before he reached the road where Jane and Isobel stood, two great eyes of flaming yellow fire sprang out from the trees at the end of the lane. Two great arms of light reached out to those small bundled figures in the middle of the road.

Ben yelled, but his voice was lost in the roar that came from the woods. Wheels spun and skidded, gripped, leapt forward. The sound of the engine rose to a shriek and a roll of thunder, filling Ben's ears and his whole body with terror.

## *Chapter Fourteen*

Ben was in the ditch. As the thunder faded and the darkness returned, he supposed he ought to consider himself lucky for still being alive. The three from Cole's Hill had got a car and they had been hiding in the copse at the end of the lane, and then when the moment was right they had tried to run him down.

And Isobel and Jane, too.

Ben wondered what he would see when his thrashing arms and kicking legs at length forced him out of this mountain of snow. Bel and Jane had been right in the middle of the road. They couldn't escape.

He forced himself to clamber up and look at the road. He didn't want to, because he was afraid of what he would find.

'Some speed!' a voice said just above his head. 'Come on, Ben. Upsydaisy!'

He might have known it. It took more than a driver to get rid of Jane. He allowed himself to be hauled out, stood upright, brushed down.

'You did look funny,' Jane said. 'As though you were trying to swim in it. Hold still, you've still got it all over your ears.'

'You leave my ears out of it,' Ben told her firmly. He looked round for Isobel and saw her standing on the other side of the road trying to see the time by her watch. Ben glanced up at the sky. Dark and cold. Just a few stars, and a promise of a moon behind the trees.

Ben shivered.

'You won't be cold long,' Isobel said. 'We've got to get moving or we'll be too late.'

They began to run, saving breath for the things that were important. Ben was thinking as his feet thudded with a steady rhythm into the ruts left by the car. Something tickled the back of his mind, like a fly caught in his hair, and he shook his head trying to dislodge it and bring it out into the open.

Something someone had said.

But he couldn't remember who had said it, or what it was.

Something that was going to make all the difference, if only he could recall it.

Meanwhile three pairs of feet kept pace and time, skirting the woods which bordered Cole's Hill and making for the stretch of road along which the car would come and where the bomb would explode.

He nearly had it then. Something to do with the bomb, and the drain under the road, and the old van. If only he could stop a minute and let himself think properly . . .

On they went. The road shone like a silver river flowing between silver banks. The moon appeared over Cole's Hill, making the ramparts round its top a solid line against the sky, brooding and mysterious.

As they turned a corner, Ben thought he saw a tattered figure move back into the shadows. He slid to a stop.

'Come on!' Isobel yelled. 'We've got to get there!'

But Jane looked over her shoulder and slowed.

'Ben?'

'I've just realised,' Ben gasped. 'We've got it all wrong.'

Isobel wheeled back. 'What's got into you, Ben?'

'St Michael. Something he said, though I didn't think at the time.'

'What?'

'Just a few words. But I bet he was right. He always is.'

'How do you know he's on our side?'

Ben lifted his shoulders. 'He's never on anybody's side except his own. That's how he keeps going. But he *knows* things.'

'He's a spy.'

'Sure. That's how he knows.'

Jane was beginning to dance about in impatience. 'Ben, what you drivelling about?'

'I saw him a moment ago. At least, I think it was him, just over there.'

Isobel gazed into the darkness. 'Not a thing.'

'No. He hopped off as soon as I caught sight of him. But just seeing him brought it back to me. He was talking about gunpowder.'

'They won't use that,' Jane snorted. 'It went out with the Ark.'

'Anything to make an explosion. What he said was 'gunpowder on the hill'. And there's where it is. Up there.'

Jane stared at him in disbelief.

'But the car is going to be down *here*, nowhere near the shepherd's hut on the hill.'

'That's the point. A dead man is no use to those thugs. They're not going to explode him at all. They're going to kidnap him, hold him to ransom. When the bomb goes off on the hill, it'll distract everybody's attention. They'll all be looking the wrong way.'

'And while they're looking up at Cole's Hill—' Jane broke in.

'The three jump out and grab him and pile him into the car and then they're off. If the police are around anywhere, they'll be up on the hill. Wrong place. See?'

Jane drew in her breath sharply. 'What do we do?'

'Just as well I brought both rockets. And just as well we've still got a bit of time.'

'Not long,' Isobel said. 'Five minutes.'

'Just enough.' Ben unwrapped the black plastic bag he had been carrying all the time and pulled out one of the big rockets. He pushed it into the snow at the side of the road, stamped it down, added more snow. Then he fumbled in his pocket for the box of matches.

The first match went out in a gust of cold air, and Ben cursed. The second, cupped in his hand, stayed alight long enough to catch the thin blue paper at the bottom of the rocket.

'Stand back!' he yelled. 'Blast off!'

The blue paper smoked and fizzed and sparkled, and then with a roar and whoosh the rocket was away, straight into the sky with a tail of yellow sparks curling out behind it. Up and up it went, as they craned their heads back to follow its flight. Then, with a report like a cannon, it burst into a great glory of blue and yellow and green stars, arcing out in all directions and ending in a series of rifle-shots.

Ben leapt back to his lanuching pad with the second rocket.

'Why two?' Jane demanded. 'They must have seen that for miles around.'

'Because that's what I arranged with Drako,' Ben told her, busy with the snow and the stick. 'One for Cole's Hill, two for the road. Well, we don't want 'em all streaming up there, do we?'

The second rocket shot into the sky. Ben let out a sigh of relief. 'I was afraid it might be a dud,' he said. 'Then we would have been in a mess.'

'What now?'

'Off the road. Quick. Those three thugs will want to know what's going on, too, and it won't take 'em long to get here. Over the hedge.'

Ben dived for the ditch, scrambled through the line of straggly hawthorn, and began to run with back bent. He could hear Jane and Isobel following, could hear their outraged cries as the thorns caught them. Well, that was their bad luck. He had to get to the old van and the drain under the road, and he had to get there fast.

The van, as he remembered, was only twenty yards off the

road. He was there almost before he realised, and he stopped dead, letting Jane and Isobel crash into him from behind.

'What . . . ?' Jane gasped.

'Shush!'

Ben gazed into the gloom of the little clearing. The moon's light shone palely through the leafless branches, making the van a square block of sharp outlines and no substance.

'Anybody there?' Isobel whispered.

Ben made no answer. There *ought* to be people about, he was thinking. One of the three would be down on the road, ready to give a signal as the car's headlights became visible half a mile back. They would have to wait a moment or two to make certain it was the right car, before the explosion on top of Cole's Hill was detonated, and then, when the car slowed, they'd all be there. Perhaps, if the van was unguarded, he might have a chance to upset their plans and set off the explosion before they were ready for it.

'Stay here!' he whispered to Jane, and began to creep across the thin spatter of snow towards the van. The back doors were open now, two rectangles of blackness with a twinkling glitter where the moon caught the edge of the glass and the chrome handle. No movement, no sound. Only his own soft footfalls in the tumbled snow.

Echoes, and the rustle of frozen twigs.

Echoes of his own footsteps.

And then, with a rush and a clatter, two figures sprang from behind the van, one short, the other tall. Ben turned to run, but there was an arm across his chest like a band of iron. He kicked backwards, felt his heel bite into flesh, heard the harsh intake of breath, kicked again. The arm slid up to his neck, began to squeeze. He put his last spurt of energy into a backward butt of his head, felt the grip on his neck weaken, wriggled free. Half-running, half-falling, he stumbled away, ducking just in time below the whistling smack of a stick which Jane was whirling round her head. Isobel's only weapon was a large icy snowball, but it found its mark.

'Down to the road!' Ben yelled.

Dead wood splintered and cracked beneath their pounding feet, snow flew from their heels. They ran as though a demon was after them, but the two men were gaining fast, hands outstretched to seize them and to choke them into silence.

Ben scrambled over the ditch, pulled Jane across, saw Isobel jump like a deer to hit the road with a floundering thump. He looked up, and from his lungs came a gasp of breath. A ghostly throng was coming towards them.

Along the road, white upon the white snow, ran a line of robed figures, flying with the speed of cheetahs on the chase. The one at the head of the column brandished a hymn-book, and his hair was a violent red, and his face shone pink in the moonlight.

'Drako!' Ben shouted. He glanced over his shoulder. Three figures, two tall and the third short, stood irresolute on the edge of the ditch, caught frozen in the attack.

Drako and his robed unholy choir rolled on, a great irresistible mass. The three dark figures by the ditch faltered, stumbled, leapt back, and a cry of triumph rose from the choir's trained throats. They poured across the ditch, cassocks flying, in pursuit of the three. Ben found himself next to Drako, yelling as loudly as any of them.

Two beams of yellow light cut through the darkness, and the roar of an engine overtopped the unmusical din. Jane was still in the middle of the road, as though turned into stone.

'It's the Bishop!' Ben called out.

'Good Lord!' Drako shouted.

'No, the Bishop.'

Drako slid to a stop, and the rest of the choir piled up in

an untidy heap behind him. Ben saw Jane at the window of the Range Rover and a moment later a tall man emerged and looked about him at the confused moonlit scene.

Jane and Isobel shouted at him, and he was carried along by a dozen pulling hands, across the ditch and into the clearing where the van still stood.

'What?' was all he was allowed to say before Ben burst in with a shout of 'There they are!', and three shadows broke cover from the van and raced towards them. The mass of the choir fell back in momentary panic, but there was no time for the Bishop to escape. Alone he stood, with his hand upheld, as though daring them to appraoch.

'Back!' he called. 'In the name of—'

But one of the men was almost upon him. Ben ran out from behind, his arms stretched forward, and caught the man at the knees. The man toppled, fell, and the Bishop's hand came down on his head with a satisfying thud.

But the other two were still in the fight. They advanced upon the Bishop, grasped his arms, bundled him forward. In vain Ben kicked at their ankles, punched his fists into their legs as he scrambled up. Suddenly all of Drako's forces surged forward to the rescue. The Bishop was carried on by a great wave of human arms and flapping robes. He was caught by the swinging door at the back of the van and cursed. His hands at last found something to hold on to. It was thin, but strong, and he put all his weight on it in order to haul himself out of the mass of pushing bodies. He was not to know that what he held was wire.

The detonator to which it was attached fell and the connection was made. For a moment, a split second, nothing happened. Then a light like the blazing of the sun filled their eyes and their heads and a throbbing roll of thunder burst and roared in their ears.

Nobody moved.

Like so many wax statues they stood, stunned into a silent

calm, watching the display of fireworks from the top of Cole's Hill. Light pulsed and seared, noise banged and rumbled.

Then the wax statues came to life. Feet pounded, legs worked like pistons.

'They've escaped!' Ben yelled in an agony.

Three black figures raced, sprawling beetles against the steep white side of Cole's Hill.

'We'll get 'em!' Drako promised. It was better than Evensong any day.

The white ghosts gathered in array, and Ben and Jane and Isobel ran at their head, fighting the snow which wrapped their feet and stung their hands. Beyond the line of trees they came. Above them the three black beetles were nearing the top of the first rampart.

'We'll lose them up there,' Isobel cried.

'No!' Ben yelled. He had no breath left to say any more.

Grimly they fought on, knowing that every second widened the gap. Ben looked up. Against the glow which came from the shepherd's hut now circled with flames, the three black figures stood for a moment, then were gone.

'They're in the ditch,' Ben called out. 'Spread out!'

They attacked the steep slope of the rampart with renewed energy, and stood at last, panting, on the top. For a moment they could not see their quarry, then Ben spotted them just disappearing round a bend. At once the whole army was after them, intent on capture.

As they came to the bend, two solid beams of light shot out to meet them, and in that brilliance the three were caught.

'Watch out!' Drako yelled. 'It's the Bishop. He's driving that thing like a maniac!'

The Range Rover, having climbed the slope, was now racing towards them along the bottom of the wide ditch. They flung themselves on to the ramparts, as the three men turned and ran back in their direction, arms flying. As the Range Rover thundered past, Ben caught sight of the Bishop's face. He looked as though he was enjoying himself.

'Blast!' Ben said.

Before the men could scramble out of the way, another beam of light cut off their retreat. The two vehicles, rushing towards each other, skidded to a halt with barely two yards between them. And in those two yards the three men stood transfixed, like butterflies stuck with a pin to a board. From the second car poured a crowd of men, large, solid, dressed in blue uniforms.

But the three still had one last chance. They pounded up the slope of the second rampart, away from the clutching hands of the police straight at the assembled might of St Aldate's choir. As one man, the choir gathered itself for a spring. The three men veered, twisted, yelled, but it was too late. The choir was on them, and they were rolling, a great tumbled mass of flying arms and legs. Ben, with Drako by his side, was in the thick of it. When the world stopped turning over and over, he glanced up and saw the Bishop looking down at them.

'Dear me,' the Bishop said.

The police pulled the pieces of the puzzle apart and handcuffed the three who could now only gasp for breath. The choir, brushing snow from their robes, lined up.

'Just as well,' the Bishop remarked, 'that I had chains on my tyres, or I don't think I would have made it. Now. If you are the St Aldate's choir, why are you not singing?'

Drako's mouth fell open, but no sound came.

'I think,' the Bishop went on, 'we shall make better progress to Evensong under the influence of music. Good King Wenceslas would seem apt. When the snow lay round about, deep and crisp and even.'

'Yeah,' said Drako, pulling himself together with a visible effort, 'and all that jazz.'

The choir's voices faded into the frosty air as they processed down Cole's Hill.

Ben looked back at the smouldering ruins of the shepherd's hut, and then down to the sparkling lights of the village below. He supposed that he owed it to Drako to go and listen to the choir singing . . .

Jane was staring at the police car which with its full complement was slithering down the slope.

'Who told them?' she asked.

'Does it matter?' Isobel replied. 'Just as well they turned up when they did.'

'We could have managed,' Ben said. 'What's that over there?'

Something tattered, like a badly wrapped parcel, flapped at them from the top of the rampart.

'The blessing of Heaven,' a voice chuckled out of the darkness.

'St Michael! I thought you'd be around somewhere. I suppose it was you who phoned the police?'

The voice chuckled again. 'The angels above have their ways and means,' St Michael said, 'but at times they need a little assistance. I'll drop by tomorrow and you can repay me for the call.' The tattered figure waved and was gone.

The tune of Good King Wenceslas still floated up from below.

'Come on,' Ben said. 'Brightly shone the moon that night—'

'It'll go back in if it hears the noise you're making,' Isobel told him, but Ben went on singing. It was the wrong verse, but he didn't care about that.

**Fiction** from Granada in paperback.

---

**Holly Hobbie** Richard Dubleman £1.25 ☐
The exciting adventures of Liz Dutton who, with her magical friend Holly Hobbie, wrestles with the dangers of the Guatemalan jungle to save her father.

---

**Ivory City** Marcus Crouch 95p ☐
A collection of Indian folk tales.

---

**The Trumpeter of Krakov** Agnes Szudek 85p ☐
A collection of Polish folk tales.

---

**War of the Computers** Granville Wilson 85p ☐
A.D. 2010 and a global war breaks out between the computers which govern Earth.

**The Terror Cubes** 85p ☐
A.D. 2050 and renegade robots threaten to take over Mankind's society.

---

*Trebizon Series* Anne Digby

**First Term at Trebizon** 85p ☐
**Second Term at Trebizon** 95p ☐
**Summer Term at Trebizon** 85p ☐
**Boy Trouble at Trebizon** 95p ☐
**More Trouble at Trebizon** 85p ☐
**The Tennis Term at Trebizon** 85p ☐
**Summer Camp at Trebizon** 95p ☐
**Into the Fourth at Trebizon** 95p ☐

An exciting new modern school series about Rebecca Mason and her five friends at boarding school.

---

**The Big Swim of the Summer** Anne Digby 60p ☐
Sara seems all set to win the big swimming race until she gets involved with the strange new girl at Hocking School.

---

**Bambi's Children Part One** Felix Salten 60p ☐
**Bambi's Children Part Two** 60p ☐
**Fifteen Rabbits** 65p ☐
Three books of classic and much loved animal stories.

---

**Shadows in the Pit** Robin Chambers 70p ☐
A tense and exciting science fiction adventure.

---

D881

**Activity and Non-fiction Books** from Granada.

| | | |
|---|---|---|
| **Peter Eldin** | | |
| Match Play | 85p | ☐ |
| **Weston/Spooner** | | |
| Oxford Children's Dictionary | £2.95 | ☐ |
| **Richard Garrett** | | |
| File on Spies | 95p | ☐ |
| File on Forgers | 95p | ☐ |
| Jailbreakers | £1.25 | ☐ |
| **Margaret Crush** | | |
| Handy Homes for Creepy Crawlies | 95p | ☐ |

**Verse and Rhyme** from Granada

| | | |
|---|---|---|
| **Deborah Manley** (ed) | | |
| Funny Poems | 85p | ☐ |
| **Cyril Fletcher** (ed) | | |
| Odes and Ends | 90p | ☐ |
| **Jennifer Mulherin** (ed) | | |
| Old Fashioned Nursery Rhymes | £1.25 | ☐ |

D5A81